GOD IS IN THE SMALL STUFF AT CHRISTMAS

BRUCE & STAN

GOD IS IN THE
SMALL STUFF
AT CHRISTMAS

BRUCE & STAN

BARBOUR
PUBLISHING

Published by Barbour Publishing, Inc., P.O. Box 719, Uhrichsville, Ohio 44683, www.barbourbooks.com

Our mission is to publish and distribute inspirational products offering exceptional value and biblical encouragement to the masses.

ᴇᴄᴘᴀ Member of the
Evangelical Christian
Publishers Association

Printed in the United States of America.

CONTENTS

INTRODUCTION

There is no season more wonderful, no time of year more anticipated, and no celebration more meaningful than Christmas. You love Christmas. We know that because you are reading a book *about* Christmas.

The signs and traditions of Christmas are unmistakable: Christmas lights on every corner, Christmas music on every radio station, frantic shopping, gift giving and gift getting, church services and pageants—the list goes on.

In the midst of this flurry of activity, many of us try to remember the *reason* for Christmas. We do our best to stay focused on (or at least occasionally reminded of) the fact that Christmas celebrates the birth of Christ. We attempt to reflect on the history, the symbols, and the spiritual meaning of Christmas that transcends the commercialism.

Keeping Christ in Christmas—or even *finding* Him in the holiday hubbub—can be difficult. And not just because some have done their best to obliterate the religious significance of Christmas. All cultural and political arguments aside, we simply live a fast-paced life at Christmastime, and God often gets moved to the background. None of us wants that to happen—it's just an unfortunate reality of the season. But it doesn't have to be that way.

Perhaps we need to see Christ in more than just the church pageant or the nativity scene on the mantel. Is it possible to see Jesus in the other traditions and symbols of Christmas? We think so, and that's why we've written this book. It is our sincere desire that Christ may be more prominent in your holiday celebrations as you learn to experience Him in all the details of Christmas.

Each chapter in this book addresses a single element of the Christmas story or a particular tradition or symbol of the season. Some of them may appear to be trivial; a few of them might seem entirely secular with no underlying spiritual significance. We haven't tried to extract religious symbolism when it isn't there. But we have tried to put things into a historical, cultural, or seasonal context that will allow you to use the images of the Christmas season as a reminder of the God of Christmas.

It is our prayer that the hectic pace of your life this Christmas will slow enough that you can see God in the details of the season. Reminders of His presence are all around you. You'll enjoy Christmas all the more when Christ is at the center of your celebration.

This is how Jesus the Messiah was born.

MATTHEW 1:18

ONE

THE STORY OF CHRISTMAS

Christmas is nothing if not a story. To be sure, it's more than a story (as we will see throughout this book), but it is not any less.

Most likely you have been aware of the Christmas story your whole life. You could probably tell it with a great deal of accuracy without once looking in the Bible, where the Christmas story is prominently featured. You're not alone in your familiarity. For the past two thousand years, the Christmas story has captured the imagination and devotion of billions of people in every culture. There are two reasons for this.

First, as remarkable as it seems, the Christmas story is *true*. By definition, a story is a narrative—either true or fictitious—designed to interest or instruct the hearer or reader. There are plenty of fictitious stories that have become part of the fabric of human culture. The *Iliad* and the *Odyssey* by Homer (the ancient Greek, not Homer Simpson), and the accounts of Camelot, Robin Hood, and Santa Claus are just a few examples of legendary stories with ageless appeal—because they describe human desire and drama in universal images. But even though these stories and the characters seem larger than life, they aren't true.

In the general culture, it's likely that many people just assume that the Christmas story—with its cast of well-known characters—is a made-up tale handed down through the centuries. It's a nice story, many would say, but hardly true. After all, do you really believe in such things as angels? Or a super-bright star that moved like a guiding light across the sky, helping three wise men from the East find their way across an entire continent just to honor a baby? And then there's the part about the virgin birth. That can't be true, can it?

If you already believe the Christmas story, don't take

offense if people ask such questions. They're legitimate, and it's important that we know the answers. But before we look at *why* the Christmas story is true, let's consider the alternative. What if the Christmas story were *not* true? What if it belonged on the same bookshelf as Robin Hood and Santa Claus? What difference would it make?

For one thing, the Christmas story wouldn't matter one way or the other, just like the story of Camelot doesn't matter much beyond the values of loyalty and chivalry contained in the tale. Those are important values, but you can find them in lots of stories. For another thing, if the Christmas story weren't true, it wouldn't have any power. Like the story of Santa Claus, it would fail to have much impact for anyone over the age of seven. It would be a nice story, but not one that anyone took very seriously. The fact of the matter, of course, is that the Christmas story *does* matter, and it is powerful.

The *power* of the Christmas story is the second reason why it has captured the imagination and the devotion of so many people. It tells us about God and why it was necessary for Him to reach out to His human creation in the best way possible. How was that? By sending His only Son to earth to be born of a virgin, to live a perfect life, and to make things right with God in Heaven on *our* behalf.

Yes, the Christmas story captures our imagination year after year with its drama and color and beauty and charm. But unless we see it for what it really is—a true and powerful story that matters to every person who has ever lived—then we will never connect with the living God in a meaningful way.

- All stories are meant to be told; do your best to become a Christmas storyteller.

- More important than knowing the Christmas story is true is knowing *why* it's true.

- The Christmas story is both ancient and timeless.

- Although the story of Christmas occurred in the past, it profoundly affects your future.

- Christmas is nothing without Christ.

Christmas is a time when people of all religions
come together to worship Jesus Christ.

Matt Groening (creator of The Simpsons)

TWO

GOD'S STORY

There are so many mental pictures associated with Christmas. Whether you're in snow-covered Vermont or sweltering Palm Springs, the word "Christmas" brings to mind images of:

- a decorated tree in your family room;

- that elaborate dinner set on a festive table surrounded by family members (both the normal and the abnormal);

- holiday shopping;

- the anticipation of opening Christmas cards from long-ago friends;

- the stockings hung on the mantel (which are purely decorative since people stopped giving oranges as Christmas gifts); and

- brightly wrapped gifts under the tree.

Oh, yes, and let's not forget the nativity scene.

For various reasons—apathy, vandalism, or efforts by the ACLU—you may not see a life-size nativity in your town. But you might have a miniature version of the crèche prominently displayed in your home during the yuletide season. A little manger, holding a removable baby Jesus is always in the center; then you put Mary, seated on a hay bale, beside the manger; the kneeling Joseph is placed on the other side. Surrounding them is a wobbly stable that would probably fall over had you not strategically placed a sheep and donkey to prop it up. Also nearby are a few shepherd boys in various poses.

If you purchased the deluxe nativity kit, you also have

a majestic angel with a six-inch wingspan. Since he's too heavy to place on top of the stable, you've got him taped to the wall. And the wise men, with camel, are also in the vicinity. (If you're a stickler for historical accuracy and know that the magi didn't visit Jesus until he was about two years old, you've placed the wise men, with camel, on the coffee table at the other end of the family room. That denotes their geographic distance from the manger on the night of Christ's birth.)

With the commercialization of Christmas, retailers are constantly providing a parade of paraphernalia to catch your imagination as the premier decoration for the holiday season. By its nature, the nativity scene is humble and unassuming, so it often loses out to other ornamentation with more flash and pizzazz. The status of that manger set in many homes might even be classified as "small stuff" at Christmastime.

Although it may be modest and unpretentious, the nativity scene presents the best image of Christmas. Unlike any other ornament or decoration, the manger setting—in its singular representation—conveys the essence of Christmas: that God loved the world so much that He was willing to send His Son to earth.

As you walk past the manger display in your living room,

don't be so preoccupied that you miss the significance of what it stands for. There is a great "back story" behind that collection of figurines. Don't just think of baby Jesus in a hay trough; realize that this was the Son of God who for eternity past had reigned in heaven. Imagine the celestial demotion of moving from heaven to earth, and don't overlook the indignity (and humiliation) of what He suffered when He assumed human form. (We might not consider taking on "human form" to be a cause of mortification, but it is if you are deity.)

Despite its comparatively bland appearance, the nativity scene is the premier Christmas decoration. It stands for the moment when God directly intervened into time and space to give us His Son. You don't get that kind of significance with a candy cane.

. . .IN THE SMALL STUFF

- Don't let God's presence be overshadowed by the Christmas presents.

- Thoughts of Christmas should be more God-centered than self-centered.

- The decorations in your house aren't nearly as important as the spirit of Christmas in your heart.

- It's no coincidence that Jesus was born on Christmas Day. His birth was the start of the celebration.

- Whenever the story of God's love for humanity is explained, the story of Christmas is told.

"For God so loved the world so much that he gave his one and only Son, so that everyone who believes in him will not perish but have eternal life."

JOHN 3:16

THREE

WHEN LOVE CAME DOWN

If there's one Christmas message that seems to be the most common, it's the standard, "Let there be peace on earth." Don't get us wrong: We're all for peace—on earth, in our communities, in our families, and anywhere else harmony is needed. We just happen to believe that peace isn't the central message of Christmas. True, "Peace on earth" makes for great Christmas card copy, and the angels did announce it to the shepherds on the first Christmas Eve. But there's something even more important that goes to the heart of what Christmas is all about.

In fact, we'll go so far as to say that without this "more important something," you can't have peace. Not in the world, not in your city, and for sure not in your family. You probably already know what we're talking about. It's love.

We admit that a phrase like "What the world needs now is love" doesn't sound as Christmassy as "Peace on earth." But it should, for one simple reason: Love is why we have Christmas. Don't just take our word for it. The nineteenth-century poet Christina Rossetti famously captured the spirit of love at Christmas when she wrote:

> *Love came down at Christmas,*
> *Love all lovely, love divine;*
> *Love was born at Christmas,*
> *Star and angels gave the sign.*

If that's not enough to convince you, see what the Bible says about love at Christmas:

> *God showed how much he loved us by sending his*
> *one and only Son into the world so that we might*
> *have eternal life through him.*

1 JOHN 4:9

What's interesting about this demonstration of God's love is that it isn't merely a *decision* God made. Love is an *expression* of God's character, because God in His very nature is love. That's what the Bible means when it says, "God is love" (1 John 4:8). Showing how much He loves us isn't an option for God. Love is who God *is* and love is what God *does*. The ultimate expression of God's love was His sending of Jesus into the world. Like we said, love is why we have Christmas.

When we understand that God is love, we come to realize that it is in God's nature to give of Himself. He gives to bless us, though that idea flies in the face of a common belief that God is a vengeful and grumpy deity who delights in creating misery for us poor humans. Nothing could be further from the truth.

It's easy to blame God for the problems we see in the world. It's certainly easier than blaming ourselves. But that doesn't square with reality. Rather than blaming God, we need to give Him credit for providing a solution to our problems—a solution born out of love. A solution born on Christmas.

What makes love such a powerful Christmas theme is that it doesn't stop after the holiday like a truce between warring armies. Because love comes from the heart of God to us, we have the power to share that love with others. That's what the Bible means when it says, "Dear friends, since God loved us that much, we surely ought to love each other" (1 John 4:11).

The problem with peace at Christmas is that it's a two-way street. Both parties have to agree to be nice for peace to exist. Not so with love. You don't need your unlikable neighbor or your cantankerous relative or your unreasonable boss to love you first. You can make a decision to love them preemptively with the same kind of love God shows at Christmas—and every other day of your life.

. . .In the Small Stuff

- Knowing that God is love is the first step to knowing God.

- Love is the most powerful force in the world because God is love.

- The best way to show people that God loves them is to show them love.

- Love came through Jesus at Christmas so that love could go out through you.

- God's love is the reason we have Christmas—and Jesus is the result.

"All right then, the Lord himself
will give you the sign. Look!
The virgin will conceive a child!
She will give birth to a son
and will call him Immanuel
(which means 'God is with us')."

ISAIAH 7:14

FOUR

THE PROPHETS

Long before the month of December, we are given gentle reminders of the approaching holiday season—like the Christmas carols playing on the mall's sound system beginning the day after Halloween. Nonetheless, it seems like Christmas sneaks up on us. We're never ready for it; it always comes too quickly.

The *first* Christmas caught people off guard, as well. It came almost incognito. Oh, sure, there was the star in the East, the angelic hosts, and the announcement to the shepherd boys. But nobody had marked this occasion on the calendar, and there was no pre-event publicity at the Bethlehem shopping mall. The precise date and time might have caught Mary and Joseph by surprise. (We're sure they would have preferred that the labor contractions were postponed until they had returned home to Nazareth.)

But God wasn't caught unaware by the first Christmas. It happened according to the divine plan He put in motion centuries in advance. And He hadn't kept the plan a secret. God had given the world lots of clues about the coming birth of Jesus. Through His prophets, God proclaimed unmistakable details about the Messiah's debut:

• Approximately fourteen hundred years before Christ was born, God spoke through Moses to indicate that the Savior of the world would be born of a woman and would be a descendant of Abraham.

• The prophet Isaiah, who lived around 740 BC, clearly stated that the Messiah would be in the lineage of King David.

• Isaiah also disclosed that the Messiah would be born of a virgin. Inconceivable!

• The prophet Micah, a contemporary of Isaiah, revealed that the Messiah would be born in the sleepy town of Bethlehem.

The advance notice of the coming Messiah wasn't limited to the circumstances of that first Christmas. Bible scholars point to more than forty clear prophecies that refer to the Messiah, all of which were fulfilled by Jesus Christ alone. They include:

- That His childhood would be spent in Egypt;

- That He would ride triumphantly into Jerusalem on a donkey;

- That He would suffer for the sins of the world;

- That He would be hung on a cross, but contrary to the custom, none of His bones would be broken;

- That men would gamble for His clothes;

- His exact dying words;

- That He would come back to life after death.

What are the odds that a person could fulfill *all* of the Bible prophecies about the Messiah as Jesus did? One mathematician, who calculated those odds, illustrated the answer with the following analogy: Suppose that the State of Texas, some 267,000 square miles, could be covered three feet deep with silver dollars. (He calculated it would take 7.5 trillion cubic feet of silver dollars to accomplish this task.) Only one of those silver dollars would be marked with a red X and buried randomly in the gigantic pile. Finally, a blindfolded man would be dropped from a plane anywhere over Texas and allowed to stumble around for days, knee-deep in silver dollars, before he would be allowed to select just one coin. The odds that the man would select the silver dollar with the X are the same odds as one man satisfying all the prophecies of the Messiah.

Obviously, the birth of Christ was no accident. It was no coincidence. It was no happenstance. It was no fluke or twist of fate. It was part of God's grand design that had been in the works since before the creation of the universe.

From time to time, you might wish that Christmas didn't arrive so quickly. You might feel frazzled because it seems that Christmas crept up on you and arrived inconveniently early. It might be that way with your family celebration on December 25. But the first Christmas came at the perfect time—precisely according to God's timetable.

- There are a lot of secrets around Christmastime—but the prophets announced God's gift in advance.

- The prophecies of the Messiah's birth were made in such amazing detail that there was no chance of mistaken identity.

- You don't have to worry about refunds or exchanges when you get exactly what God wants you to have.

- Aren't you glad you don't have to worry about selecting a Christmas gift fourteen hundred years in advance?

- Sadly, the Old Testament prophets knew about the gift of the Messiah but weren't around for the celebration of His arrival. But it's worse if we, who know the true meaning of Christmas, celebrate the holiday without acknowledging the Messiah.

"The Savior—yes, the Messiah,
the Lord—has been born
today in Bethlehem, the city of David!"

LUKE 2:11

FIVE

THE COMING MESSIAH

There's something about anticipation that's hard to beat. When we anticipate something—especially something really big—we tend to build it up in our mind. Sometimes, our mental build-up reaches the point that the anticipated thing, event, or person has a hard time meeting our expectations. What a let-down when that thing, event, or person doesn't quite measure up to what we had in mind.

Imagine something or someone that you once anticipated—then multiply the level of anticipation by spreading it out over fourteen hundred years or so, with each year adding to the intensity of your expectation. Now you have some idea of what the Jews—God's chosen people—were expecting when they imagined what their "Messiah" would be like.

Throughout the Old Testament, God promised the Jews that He would deliver them from their problems by sending a king to establish God's Kingdom on earth. This deliverer was referred to as "the Messiah." Moses was a great deliverer, but he never had a kingdom. In fact, no leader of Israel had a great kingdom until David came along. As the "anointed one," David was a type of messiah (the word literally means "anointed one"), but he was not *the* Messiah. Thoughtful Jews understood that no human king could fulfill the high ideal of the Messiah, who would be God coming down to earth.

After David's great earthly kingdom came to an end, the prophets of Israel began endowing the anticipated Messiah with names that clearly placed Him beyond mere mortals. He would be "Wonderful Counselor, Mighty God, Everlasting Father, Prince of Peace" (Isaiah 9:6). Furthermore, the Messiah would be:

- A direct descendant of King David (Isaiah 11:1);

- Born in Bethlehem, David's own birthplace (Micah 5:2); and

- Born of a virgin (Isaiah 7:14).

So the stage was set, and the time was right for God to send the great Deliverer to rescue His people—and that's what God did. He sent Jesus, the Messiah, the Anointed One, who was a descendant of David (Luke 1:31–33), born in Bethlehem (Luke 2:4, 6–7) and born of a virgin (Matthew 1:18, 22–23). God even sent one of His personal messengers, an angel who proclaimed on that first Christmas Eve:

> *"I bring you good news that will bring great joy to all people. The Savior—yes, the Messiah, the Lord—has been born today in Bethlehem, the city of David! And you will recognize him by this sign: You will find a baby wrapped snugly in strips of cloth, lying in a manger."*
>
> LUKE 2:10–12

There was no mistaking it. The prophecies had been fulfilled. God had come to earth in the person of Jesus. The Messiah had come. Surely the Jews would embrace their king.

There was only one problem. They were anticipating a different kind of Messiah, and the baby lying in the manger didn't measure up to their ideal. They expected a royal king born in a palace; what God sent them was a common baby born in a stable. They expected a birth announcement to be made to the religious leaders; God first told a bunch of lowly shepherds. They anticipated a conquering king who would deal with their enemies and rule politically; Jesus came to serve and to give His life for others.

It's easy to criticize the Jews for missing the real point and rejecting Jesus the Messiah. But before we do that, we need to look at ourselves and ask what kind of Deliverer we're looking for. Are we expecting Jesus to deliver us from our problems? Are we expecting Jesus to deliver us from our enemies? Are we expecting Jesus to deliver us from poverty and sickness? Jesus can do all of those things, but that's not why He came. More than anything else, Jesus the Messiah came to deliver us from our sins.

- The meaning of the name *Jesus* is "Savior," and save is exactly what He came to do.

- There have been many "messiahs" throughout history, but only one Messiah.

- The true Messiah doesn't simply meet the expectations of those looking for deliverance. He exceeds them.

- We may not understand exactly *why* Jesus came into the world, but like the angels we should be glad that He did.

- Without the coming of the Messiah, there is no Christmas.

An angel of the Lord appeared to him in a dream.
"Joseph, son of David," the angel said, "do not be
afraid to take Mary as your wife.
For the child within her was conceived by
the Holy Spirit. And she will have a son,
and you are to name him Jesus, for he will
save his people from their sins."

MATTHEW 1:20–21

SIX

THE NAMES OF JESUS

Selecting a name for a newborn child can be difficult. Most expectant parents spend many months writing lists of "boy names" and "girl names." Maybe that's why God designed the human gestation period to be nine months in duration. It usually takes that long for the mother and father to agree on mutually acceptable monikers. A lot of factors must be considered:

- How does it sound with the last name? (You can't name a baby girl "Sandy" if her last name is "Beach.")

- Did either the mother or the father date a person with this name while in high school?

- Will the bullies on the playground find the name too easy to rhyme? (Take "Meyer" off the "boy's name" list, because you don't want him called "Meyer the Cryer.")

- Is the name too old-fashioned (like "Winifred") or too hip (like "Xerox")?

Besides the phonetic sound of the baby's potential name, parents often consider the derivation and meaning behind the name. This factor is mainly promoted by the publishers of those "baby name" books. In our twenty-first century Western culture, there isn't much meaning associated with specific names. No parent really thinks about name derivations when they are yelling for *Tyler* or *Jorun* to come downstairs for dinner.

Mary and Joseph probably didn't make a list of name ideas for their baby. It isn't that they were cavalier about naming their child. Quite the contrary. The meaning of a name was a really big deal in first-century Middle Eastern culture; every utterance of that name was closely associated with its historical meaning and considered a source of power. But Mary and Joseph could focus their mental energies on the other concerns that panic expectant parents. The name of their child had been preselected.

In separate dreams, an angel had appeared to Joseph and to Mary. The angel declared that Mary would give birth to a baby boy whose name would be "Jesus." (This was another clue to Mary and Joseph that this would be no ordinary child because *Jesus* means "the Lord saves.")

And baby Jesus didn't lack for nicknames, either. About four hundred years earlier, the prophet Isaiah had declared that the child born to be the Messiah would also be known by four other distinctly royal titles. Consider what these names reveal about the kind of man the baby Jesus would become:

- *Wonderful Counselor*—"Wonderful" typically referred to supernatural, so the Messiah was one who was characterized by perfect wisdom.

- *Mighty God*—This is a term that predicted the Messiah's ultimate triumph over evil.

- *Everlasting Father*—The Messiah is a protective Father who guards His children for all eternity.

- *Prince of Peace*—He brings peace in the sense of wholeness and reconciliation with God for every person.

When Jesus was born, Mary and Joseph didn't look at Him and say, "Isn't He the cutest little Everlasting Father you have ever seen." And when Jesus was playing stickball in the streets of Nazareth as an eleven-year-old kid, nobody said, "Wow, that Wonderful Counselor can really swing the bat." And as a kid, He was probably never accused of having a Messiah complex (although those accusations were made about twenty years later). He was just plain ol' Jesus, the son of Joseph the carpenter.

But almost two thousand years later, we have the advantage of looking at His life from a retrospective vantage point. While He was just "Jesus" at birth, we have the privilege of reading the historical record of His life and resurrection. We can see that He lived up to the names that were bestowed upon Him. Think about that the next time you hear the lyrics to "Away in a Manger." That wasn't just the baby Jesus in the manger; it was the Savior of the world. And He had the names to prove it.

- Whether it's Christmastime or not, there is no name as universally recognized as "Jesus."

- If Mary and Joseph had been allowed to name their child, it might have been baby Joseph, Jr., lying in the manger.

- Most children are told to live up to their family name. Jesus was deserving of His royal titles at the moment of His birth.

- To His parents He was known as Jesus, but you can know Him as "Savior."

- The Bible says that at the name of Jesus, every knee will bow and every tongue will confess that He is Lord.

He who is the faithful witness to all these things says, "Yes, I am coming soon!" Amen! Come, Lord Jesus!

REVELATION 22:20

SEVEN

ADVENT

One of the great joys of Christmas is the arrival of special guests. It may be a son or daughter who has been away at college or in the military. It could be a favorite aunt or uncle who has flown in for the holidays. Friends might be coming to share a holiday dinner. Whoever it is, you anticipate the arrival of your guests and prepare yourself and your home for their coming. And finally, when you hear the knock or the doorbell, you jump up, eager to welcome your loved ones into your heart and home.

That spirit and emotion are at the heart of Advent, a way of celebrating Christmas that may be new to you. Perhaps you're aware of Advent but don't know a lot about what it means or what you're supposed to do about it. When you hear the word, you probably think of candles and calendars. While those are often involved in the celebration, they are merely symbols of what Advent is all about.

The word *Advent* literally means "coming" or "arrival." When related to Christmas, it has to do with the coming of Jesus Christ. It's that period of expectant waiting and preparation for the celebration of the events surrounding the birth of Jesus.

If Advent is a new concept for you, don't feel bad. In fact, be glad that you are discovering something that can help bring the true meaning of Christmas to you and your family in a fresh way. Rather than going through the Christmas season in a frenzy, pausing for just one day to contemplate and celebrate the Savior's birth, you have the opportunity to take more time to prepare your heart and mind for the commemoration of Jesus' arrival into the world.

Traditionally, there are two ways to celebrate Advent. The first is to anticipate the coming of Christ on the four Sundays leading up to Christmas Day by lighting a candle each Sunday. Each candle represents a different aspect of the Christmas story. One tradition follows various *people* of the Christmas story: the prophets, Mary, the angels, and the shepherds. Another tradition emphasizes four *emotions* of Christmas: hope, peace, love, and joy.

Whether you follow the people or the emotions of Christmas, you celebrate Advent by lighting a candle on each of the four Sundays before Christmas—and taking time to think about what it represents. If you're doing this with your family, you can share the meaning of Christmas together and talk about why the prophets are part of the story, or why Christmas inspired hope. With either tradition, there is always a fifth candle, called a "Christ candle," that is lit on Christmas Eve or Christmas Day to signify Jesus' birth.

The second way to celebrate Advent is with an Advent calendar. There's nothing sacred about the calendar itself (just as there's nothing sacred about the candles), but like the candles, a calendar can help you think about what's sacred. The Advent calendar allows you to mark off each day of December leading up to Christmas. As you might expect, Advent calendars have twenty-four spaces or boxes, each one containing a special image of a person, symbol, or emotion of Christmas. You can buy these calendars ready-made or make them yourself. Whichever you choose, it's a wonderful way to engage children to think about Christmas beyond the secular images of presents and Santa Claus that bombard them throughout the season.

Perhaps one of the greatest benefits of the Advent celebration—whether you use candles or a calendar or both—is that it reminds us that the coming of Christ into the world is not something that happened just once in the *past*. Advent tells us that Christ continues to come into our world in the *present* through the lives of people who choose to follow Him. And it also reminds us that Jesus is coming again in the *future* in the Second Advent.

Just as we delight in preparing for special guests to our physical home, we need to be preparing our spiritual house for the arrival of the most special Guest of all.

- Unless we choose to bring the meaning of Christmas to our celebrations, we will miss the meaning altogether.

- There's something about waiting that prepares us for arrival.

- Christmas is a time of contrasting emotions: hope and despair, peace and conflict, togetherness and loneliness. Advent helps put them in perspective.

- Getting on and getting off the holiday fast track have this in common: They are both choices.

- We will never recognize the significance of Christmas until we slow down enough to think about it.

Faith is the confidence that what we hope
for will actually happen;
it gives us assurance about things we cannot see.

HEBREWS 11:1

EIGHT

HOPE

Christmas is a season of hope and wonder, but not for the reasons you think:

- Most kids have a particular gift they *hope* for, and they *wonder* if they are going to get it.

- A wife has the *hope* that her husband will get her a romantic gift, but she realistically *wonders* what electrical appliance she'll receive from him.

- We all *hope* not to get another fruitcake from the relatives, and when it arrives, we *wonder* if they will recognize it later in the backyard garden as a decorative boulder.

In these contexts, *hope* is merely a form of wishing. But the true spirit of hope at Christmastime has a much deeper and richer meaning. The *hope of Christmas* denotes an expectation with certainty. Christmas hope is a confident assurance that something will happen. It is a hope that you can hang on to when the rest of life seems shaky.

Christmas hope is thousands of years old, rooted in the history of the Jews. God had promised them a Messiah who would be their deliverer. They relied on this hope when they were enslaved by Pharaoh in Egypt (about 1700 BC). The promise of the Messiah also sustained them during the invasion of Israel when many of them were taken captive and transported to Assyria (about 700 BC) and when Jerusalem was destroyed and the Jews were exiled to Babylon (about 600 BC). And, during the earthly lifetime of Jesus, with the Jews suffering under the tyranny of the Roman government, they anxiously waited for the Messiah to lead a political revolt.

The birth of Christ—what we celebrate as *Christmas*—was

the fulfillment of God's promise to send a Messiah. But few people recognized it as that. Their oversight is understandable. They were expecting the arrival of a conquering hero. They didn't imagine that their Deliverer would come dressed in a diaper. They wanted to see Him standing tall, holding a sword in His outstretched hand. They weren't expecting an infant squirming in a hay-strewn feeding trough.

Even when He grew to be a man, few people recognized Jesus as the Messiah. The people wanted relief from Roman oppression, but Christ told them how to be free from sin and guilt. They wanted financial prosperity, but Christ spoke of success in terms of being reconciled with God. They wanted political peace, but Jesus offered spiritual peace. He wasn't what they were looking for—but the fact remains that God delivered on His promise to send what they needed, whether they realized it or not.

Now, about two thousand years later, God is still in the promise-keeping business. The Bible contains promises that God has made and not forgotten:

- You can turn to Him in times of crisis;

- He will provide for you in times of need;

- He loves you as His own child.

Skeptics might say that these are empty promises—nothing more than wishful thinking. But the hope of Christmas proves the skeptics wrong. These are the promises of the same God who made good on His pledge to send a Messiah. The God who invaded earth with His presence on that first Christmas night to fulfill His promise is the same God who can fulfill His promises to you.

God has proven Himself to be reliable. He can be trusted. Though the difficulties of life might make you question God's faithfulness, He is a worthy recipient of your hope. Maybe that is one reason He's given us the hope of Christmas. It is a perennial reminder that God keeps His promises. And you can hang your hope on that.

. . .IN THE SMALL STUFF

- The birth of Jesus was God making good on His promises.

- You can have hope in the future because of what God has done in the past.

- Wishing is for Santa Claus; hope is for Christ.

- God's gift of what you need may arrive wrapped in a package that you don't recognize.

- The hope of Christmas is the confident assurance that God is in control and knows what He's doing.

This is a record of the ancestors of Jesus the Messiah,
a descendant of David and of Abraham.

MATTHEW 1:1

NINE

THE ANCESTRY OF JESUS

Have you ever wondered what your ancestors were like? Maybe you've studied your family tree to get a portrait of your heritage. It can be a revealing exercise, because your past can shed a lot of light on your present.

Most people who follow Jesus know a fair amount about His life on earth—His miracles, His teachings, His death and resurrection. But they know very little about His past. That's probably because few people think Jesus *had* a past, at least a past on earth. Most people, if they've given the topic any thought at all, probably believe the life of Jesus on earth started when He came down from heaven to be born in Bethlehem, and concluded about thirty-three years later when He returned to heaven.

It would be easy to conclude this if all we had were the Gospels of Mark and John. These two biographies of Jesus start with Jesus as an adult. But those are just two of the four books about the life of Christ in the New Testament. If you read Matthew and Luke, not only do you find a description of the birth of Christ, but a record of His ancestry, as well.

In fact, Matthew starts with the ancestry of Jesus, telling us right off the bat that Jesus was a descendant of both David and Abraham. This detail is significant because God made promises to each man: that one of Abraham's descendants would bless the whole world (Genesis 12:2–3) and one of David's would establish an eternal kingdom (2 Samuel 7:12–13). In both cases that person turned out to be Jesus.

In Matthew's genealogy, Jesus is presented as the legal male descendant of David, through adoption by Joseph, making Him heir to King David's eternal throne. To anyone seeking a legal qualification for Jesus as Messiah, this list of ancestors is all they need.

But Matthew doesn't stop there. While he's careful to present Jesus as the ultimate and perfect fulfillment of the promise God made to David (that his kingdom would go on forever), Matthew also shows that the ancestors of Jesus were very human. True, the cast of characters (which spans two thousand years) includes some heroes of the faith, such as Abraham, Isaac, and David. But most of the ancestors in the human bloodline of Jesus were quite ordinary, and some—Rahab and Tamar stand out— had less than sterling reputations. Others were downright nasty. In other words, the ancestry of Jesus isn't all that different than yours or ours.

Why was Jesus, the Son of God, born into such a "human" family? Because Jesus came to earth to save *all* people: kings and heroes, ordinary people and scoundrels, honest people and thieves. When we look at the ancestry of Jesus—something we tend to skip over in order to get to the story of Jesus' life—we can see that His past impacts our present and our future.

For all of us living two millennia after the birth of Jesus,

His ancestry assures us that God has always worked through all kinds of people to accomplish His purposes. It also tells us that He can work through us *now*, regardless of where we came from or where we fit on the family tree.

. . .IN THE SMALL STUFF

- Knowing where you came from can tell you a lot about who you are.

- Knowing where Jesus came from can tell you a lot about who He is.

- The deity of Jesus means He can save us. The humanity of Jesus means He understands us.

- The eternal kingdom of Jesus has already begun in the hearts of those who love and follow Him.

- God wants to use you, no matter who you are or where you come from.

But the angel said, "Don't be afraid, Zechariah!
God has heard your prayer.
Your wife, Elizabeth, will give you a son, and you are
to name him John. He will prepare the people for the
coming of the Lord."

LUKE 1:13, 17

TEN

ELIZABETH AND ZECHARIAH

There are only a few choice roles in the typical Christmas pageant. The "baby Jesus" is usually portrayed by a doll, because the church insurance policy doesn't cover injury to infants placed precariously in a cardboard manger. The starring male and female roles are "Joseph" and "Mary." Next in the pecking order are the wise men, because of their flamboyant costumes. (These can be portrayed by boys or girls, because all gender identity is lost with false mustaches and beards glued onto young faces under Burger King crowns.) For the theatrically challenged, the girls are assigned to "the angelic hosts," and every boy wearing a bathrobe and a dish towel on his head gets the part of a shepherd.

The always-omitted characters of the Christmas story are Zechariah and Elizabeth. The Gospel of Luke tells the story of this elderly couple, devout and obedient followers of God. Although Zechariah was an honored priest who worked in the temple in Jerusalem, the couple carried the personal pain and social stigma of being childless. In the Jewish culture, infertility was equated with a lack of God's blessing on a couple's life.

The angel Gabriel appeared to Zechariah to inform him that Elizabeth would give birth to a son. This miracle baby, born to a woman well past her childbearing years, would be named John, the angel said, and would persuade many Jews to turn to God. Call him a PR man of sorts for the Messiah's arrival. (If you're familiar with the story, you know that this "John" was John the Baptist—an occupational nickname, not a reference to his denominational affiliation.)

It's a toss-up whether Zechariah was more excited about seeing the Messiah in his lifetime or about having a son who would be the advance man for the Messiah. But despite his devotion and his excitement, Zechariah let his practicality get the best of him.

In an honest moment of doubt, he asked Gabriel whether it was possible to roll back the biological clock for himself and his wife. Angels, who probably see miracles on a regular basis, apparently get a little exasperated with human frailties. Because of Zechariah's initial doubt, the angel took away the old priest's ability to speak.

Zechariah must have been pretty competent at charades and shorthand for the next nine months because, despite being mute, he managed to inform Elizabeth of all of the angel's details. The physical aspects of Zechariah's wild tale were confirmed when Elizabeth became pregnant. And the theological aspects were confirmed when Elizabeth, six months into her pregnancy, received a visit from a much younger, and recently engaged, relative by the name of Mary. When Mary walked into the room, Elizabeth's baby jumped in the womb. Elizabeth correctly understood this to be a sign that Mary would be the mother of the Messiah. In about thirty years, baby John would become a prophet for the baby Jesus.

When Elizabeth gave birth, she announced that the baby boy would be named John. Family members pressured her to name the kid "Zechariah, Jr.," but Daddy boldly scribbled, "His name is John!" At that moment, the voice of Zechariah was restored and the new parents celebrated their son's birth and future ministry.

The experience of Zechariah and Elizabeth tells a comforting story for those of us who doubt God from time to time. It is a picture of how God answers our prayers—even those that may have been long abandoned. It shows that God works through the lives of those who are available to Him, even if they have honest doubts and hesitations. We should be encouraged that our limitations do not restrict God's power. He can accomplish His will through us, even if we don't understand just what's going on.

So if you know a young boy who lacks acting ability—but who's still disappointed at being cast as a shepherd in the Christmas pageant—tell him to request the role of Zechariah. And remind the director that for the most part this is a nonspeaking role.

- Christmas is a time of miracles, so don't doubt that God has the ability to perform one for you.

- Aren't you glad that God doesn't abandon His plans as quickly as you quit praying?

- Maybe God wants to do something so miraculous in your life that it will leave you speechless.

- God welcomes honest doubt—but is displeased with disobedience. Don't let the former turn into the latter.

- Time is not an obstacle to God's power. Don't let it be an obstacle to your prayers.

The next day John saw Jesus coming
toward him and said,
"Look! The Lamb of God who takes away
the sin of the world!"

John 1:29

ELEVEN

JOHN THE BAPTIST

Have you ever wondered why Jesus came to earth when He did? Why two thousand years ago? Why not three thousand years ago? Why not one thousand? What was so special about the world at that particular time that necessitated the coming of Jesus?

The only satisfactory answer is that the timing was perfect from God's perspective. The scriptures even tell us: "But when the right time came, God sent his Son" (Galatians 4:4). Of course, now that we have the perspective of history, we can look back and see that it was a great time for Jesus to come. Thanks to the cultural influence of the Greeks, there was a common language in the world, enabling the word of mouth about Jesus to spread quickly. Because of the military might of the Roman Empire, there was peace throughout the world, allowing the people who would later follow Jesus to disperse and tell others, using an elaborate transportation system built by the Romans.

And, perhaps most important of all, there were certain key people in place who made it their business to spread the good news about Jesus to a world very much in need of a Savior. Among those key people was a rather colorful fellow by the name of John, who you already know something about. Because he had a habit of dipping people in the water, he became known as "the baptizer," or simply, John the Baptist.

There's quite a bit of information about John in the Gospels. We know, for example, that he sported some crazy clothes, called the wilderness home, and survived on a rather unusual lo-cal diet of locusts and wild honey. We also know that even though he had no real authority, people listened to him. What they heard was a stirring message about the Lamb of God coming to take away the sins of the world. John also was a sharp critic of the religious leaders of the day, who had come to rely on their own traditions and status rather than God and His Word.

You would think that, with his idiosyncrasies and rather forceful personality, John the Baptist would have drawn a lot of attention to himself—like a modern-day rock star who turns his weirdness into fame. Well, John did attract attention all right, but his purpose was never self-serving. Far from it. John lived full-out for Jesus. In fact, Jesus was his purpose for living.

You won't find John in any Christmas pageants, and he is rarely mentioned in the traditional Christmas story. But he is right in the middle of it, and not only because he was born around the time of Jesus. Without John the Baptist, the message of Jesus and what He came to do would not have spread as quickly as it did. Without John the Baptist, the religious authorities may not have known *why* Jesus posed such a threat to their way of life. Without John the Baptist, the people who eventually followed Jesus would not have understood why Jesus came when He did.

The Christmas story has a lot of characters who inspire us to improve our lives. Mary and Joseph are examples of obedience in the face of uncertainty. The angels teach us about praise. The wise men show that it's better to give than to receive. But one character, rarely mentioned, gives us the most important message of all: A Savior has come to earth, and we need to prepare for His coming into our hearts.

- John the Baptist was unique, but he didn't make uniqueness his goal. His purpose for living was Jesus.

- God has made each of us unique, not to draw attention to ourselves, but to draw others to Jesus.

- The story of John the Baptist reminds us that God delights in choosing unlikely people to accomplish His purposes.

- Don't be afraid to speak the truth, even if it makes people uncomfortable.

- Always speak the truth in love.

Gabriel appeared to her and said,
"Greetings, favored woman! The Lord is with you!
Don't be afraid, Mary," the angel told her,
"for you have found favor with God!
You will conceive and give birth to a son,
and you will name him Jesus.
He will be very great and will be called
the Son of the Most High.
The Lord God will give him the
throne of his ancestor David.
And he will reign over Israel forever;
his Kingdom will never end!"

LUKE 1:28, 30–33

TWELVE

MARY

Mary has been praised throughout history, but her own generation wasn't too kind to her. Imagine the scandal. A young woman (possibly sixteen years of age) who became pregnant outside of marriage. In that time and culture, her situation was disastrous. Imagine the pressure and stress that Mary endured—not to mention the comments.

- First of all, who would believe her alibi? An angel appeared to her. (Yeah, right. How convenient that the angel came alone to her at night, so nobody else could confirm the sighting.)

- And the theological aspects of her story seemed preposterous: She is going to give birth to the Messiah? (Sure. God is selecting a young, obscure girl out of poverty from the hick town of Nazareth to be the birth mother of divine royalty.)

- The physiological side of her story was equally incredible: She became pregnant because the "Holy Spirit came upon her." (An immaculate conception? This story is inconceivable! If she's actually pregnant, then she's a tramp. But if it turns out that she isn't pregnant, maybe she's just insane.)

But the gossip mill in her hometown of Nazareth wasn't the worst part. She had to tell Joseph that she was pregnant, and he knew that he wasn't the father. Imagine the suspense as she waited for his reaction. Would he call off their engagement? If he abandoned her, she would certainly be a social reject the rest of her life; no one would marry her. Mary's only recourse would be to turn to her own father, but even he might cast her out of his household in disgrace. She had seen women in this plight living on the outskirts of town, and they had only two career choices: prostitution or begging.

When viewed in this light, being "favored" by God doesn't seem so special, does it? But perhaps that's the lesson God is trying to teach us through the life story of Mary. God's blessings don't exactly translate into a life of fame and fortune, peace and prosperity. To the contrary, from the time she was confronted by Gabriel, she probably encountered more pain than pleasure.

- At the outset, there was the scandal of her out-of-wedlock pregnancy.

- Then there came the difficult circumstances of using a stable as a delivery room.

- Then, when King Herod issued a decree to kill all Jewish baby boys, Mary and Joseph packed up the baby Jesus and became fugitives, escaping to Egypt.

- As her son grew into manhood, Mary lived with the

constant reminder that the ancient prophet Isaiah had predicted that the Messiah would be tortured. She knew her son was the one the prophets referred to as the "suffering servant." She lived with the unabating, penetrating pain of knowing that her son would be slaughtered for the sins of the world.

- And she was an eyewitness to crucifixion.

Yet Mary didn't hesitate to accept God's plan for her life. There is no indication that she ever complained or cursed God for the circumstances she endured as part of His plan. Quite the contrary. Her response to Gabriel was a resounding, "I am the Lord's servant. May everything you have said about me come true" (Luke 1:38).

At Christmastime it's customary for people to gather in prayer and thank the Lord for His favor and many blessings. But the story of Mary suggests that His favor may involve putting us through difficult circumstances in order to accomplish His plans. Are we truly willing servants, ready to accept whatever He wants? Maybe it takes that attitude to realize that we are blessed with God's favor simply by His love for us.

- It can take an eternal perspective to find God's blessings in our present circumstances.

- The essence of God's grace is His favor. Mary had God's favor, and so do you.

- You'll miss out on many of God's blessings if you don't expect to find them in the midst of difficulties.

- God loves you so much that He'll allow you to endure hardship.

- If you think that wealth and prosperity are the only sure signs of God's blessing, then Satan has done a good job of brainwashing you.

"Glory to God in highest heaven."

Luke 2:14

THIRTEEN

GLORY

If you were to make a list of your favorite things about Christmas, would you include "glory"? You'd probably have things like joy, peace, love, gifts, miracles, and lights in your Top Ten. (Hopefully, you would not include whiskers on kittens and warm woolen mittens.) But would *glory* be in the mix?

We certainly would not have included it in our list, but that was before we did a little research. What we found was that not only does *glory* characterize the spirit of Christmas as much as any other word, but it probably is one of the best Christmas words out there.

For one thing, you find glory throughout the biblical account of what happened at Christmas. Mary gave God glory in response to the news that she would bear the Savior of the world (Luke 1:46). When the angels announced to the shepherds that Jesus had been born, they sang out, "Glory to God in highest heaven" (Luke 2:14). And when the apostle John wrote about Jesus, he said, "And we have seen his glory, the glory of the Father's one and only Son" (John 1:14).

Truth is, glory is all over the Christmas account. So why don't we talk more about it? We suspect it has something to do with the word itself. We're uncomfortable with people who seek glory. An athlete who draws attention to himself is sometimes called a "glory hound." Someone assigned to a project who takes all the credit is said to "want all the glory." The bottom line is that we don't like people who like glory.

But that's because we're talking about *people*. The kind of glory referred to in the Bible, especially in the Christmas story, is glory directed to *God*. And that's an entirely different matter. Human glory is usually related to *performance*, but God's glory has to do with His *person*. The reason scripture tells us to give God glory is not because He needs it to feed His ego—it's because

God by definition is *glorious* and worthy of all the glory we can give Him. When applied to God, glory simply means "honor" or "excellence." Even more, it implies that God's character is perfect (Romans 3:23).

Because God is spirit, we can't see Him. But we can see the created brightness that surrounds God as He reveals Himself to us. For one thing, God reveals Himself through His creation: A brilliant sunset, a flash of lightning, and the canopy of stars above are nature's way of giving God glory (Psalm 104:2). In another more specific and even more powerful way, the invisible God has revealed Himself through the visible person of Jesus Christ, who is the light of the world (John 8:12).

This is why glory belongs in the Christmas story. The Bible says God became a human in the form of Jesus, also called the living Word, in order to show His glory to the world:

> *So the Word became human and made his home among us. He was full of unfailing love and faithfulness. And we have seen his glory, the glory of the Father's one and only Son.*

> JOHN 1:14

Just what does all this glory mean to us? How does it impact our lives, especially in the everyday small stuff of life? Quite simply, God created us so we could reflect God's glory. To put it another way, God made us to make Him look good. Even as the beauty of nature makes its Creator look good, our purpose is to make God look good by doing those things He wants us to do, especially during this season of glory.

- Giving glory to God in the highest means just that—giving God the highest place in our lives.

- When we make God look good through our lives, our words, and our actions, we glorify Him.

- Seeking glory for yourself is human; giving glory to God is divine.

- On our own, we fall short of God's glory—but with Jesus we meet His glorious standard.

- Because Jesus reveals God's glory to the world, He is the world's true light.

This is how Jesus the Messiah was born. His mother, Mary, was engaged to be married to Joseph. But before the marriage took place, while she was still a virgin, she became pregnant through the power of the Holy Spirit. Joseph. . .decided to break the engagement quietly. As he considered this, an angel of the Lord appeared to him in a dream. "Joseph, son of David," the angel said, "do not be afraid to take Mary as your wife. For the child within her was conceived by the Holy Spirit. And she will have a son, and you are to name him Jesus, for he will save his people from their sins." When Joseph woke up, he did as the angel of the Lord commanded and took Mary as his wife. But he did not have sexual relations with her until her son was born.

MATTHEW 1:18–21, 24–25

FOURTEEN

JOSEPH

Joseph was just an ordinary guy who—in God's design—got caught up in the most extraordinary events in human history. He wasn't seeking notoriety or a place in history. He was just a regular Joe (pun intended) who wouldn't have suspected that he had the qualifications to be the stepfather of the Son of God.

Joseph wasn't superspiritual. He certainly lacked the credentials of Zechariah, who held a prominent position as priest in the temple in Jerusalem. The Bible describes Zechariah and his wife, Elizabeth, as "righteous in God's eyes" (Luke 1:6). That's a pretty good endorsement etched in the pages of scripture. It doesn't mean they were perfect, but it does imply that they were sincere in their love of God, and that their obedience to God was motivated out of love for Him.

It doesn't appear that Joseph had this kind of reputation in his community. He most likely was a God-fearing man who tried with relative success to be obedient to God. (It's doubtful that Mary's father would have sanctioned the engagement to his daughter if Joseph had been a religious slacker.) Maybe Joseph volunteered for janitorial duty at his synagogue on Thursday nights—but it's likely that no one would have called him a spiritual pillar of the community.

Joseph wasn't particularly successful, and certainly not prosperous. He was a tradesman in a rural town. His town of Nazareth was little more than a pit stop on a trade route between much better places. Its roads were dusty and its people were crusty. It wasn't held in high regard. So Joseph was a nobody in a nowhere town. In a culture that had clearly-defined socioeconomic separations, Joseph became engaged to a young girl from a poor family. That tells us that his net worth was pretty paltry. If there was a flourishing business in Nazareth, it wasn't Joseph's carpentry shop.

Other than his lineage and his residency, the Bible gives only one other background clue about this Joseph: He was a just man. That tells us he was fair and attempted to do the right thing. His gesture to quietly release the pregnant Mary from their engagement contract—rather than following the tradition of putting her through a public humiliation—is evidence of his honor. This is an admirable virtue, but it makes for a short resume if you're applying to adopt the baby Messiah.

But in God's paradigm, credentials, qualifications, and past accomplishments are basically irrelevant. God is more interested in your attitude about serving Him. And in this category, Joseph was stellar. The Bible captures the essence of Joseph's heart for God with this single sentence: "When Joseph woke up, he did what the angel of the Lord commanded" (Matthew 1:24).

That's what God is looking for. Ordinary people who simply obey when God calls them. Joseph was not asked to assume an easy assignment. But he didn't try to dodge the work by pleading unworthiness or incompetence. He didn't protest or try to negotiate the terms of the task. He didn't suggest the names of others who could do a better job. He simply responded in the manner that God had requested.

God hasn't changed His tactics in the last two thousand years. He's still looking for ordinary people to be part of His extraordinary plan. He isn't recruiting the best qualified and most successful candidates. He specializes in using obscure people with obedient hearts. He wants to use people who—like Joseph—will wake up and do what He commands.

When Joseph woke up after his dream, he took a mighty leap outside his comfort zone. He could not imagine the consequences that would follow his obedience. But that didn't stop him. He didn't delay his response to take an inventory of all of his emotional feelings and gut reactions. He simply acted in obedience to God's call. Now *that* is something to put on a résumé.

- God cares more about your attitude than your aptitude.

- We should be more concerned about hearing God's call than the consequence that may befall.

- If you think that you are worthy to serve God, your ego disqualifies you from doing so.

- When you know you are incapable without God, then there is little argument about who should get the credit for the accomplishment.

- God often leads you to a destination you can't see from your current location. You'll only get a better idea of where He is taking you *after* you start moving.

Mary responded, "I am the Lord's servant.
May everything you have said about me come true."

LUKE 1:38

FIFTEEN

FAITH

If you would argue that the Christmas story requires a lot of faith, we would agree—but not for the reason you might think. If by "faith" you mean "blind faith"—because there's just no way to know for sure that the events on that first Christmas happened the way the Bible says they did—that's not what we mean. It doesn't take any more faith to believe the historic fact that Jesus was born than it does to believe the historic fact that George Washington crossed the Delaware River. In both cases we have reliable information based on trustworthy witnesses, giving us good reason to believe these events happened—even though we weren't there to see them ourselves.

On the other hand, if by "faith" you refer to the action required on our part to act on what we know to be true, then we are on the same page.

You see, it's one thing to believe that Jesus was born on Christmas Day and quite another matter to live your life as if this were actually true. By way of example, think about an airplane. You can have faith that a certain airplane will fly, but until you actually get on board and demonstrate your confidence in the plane, your faith doesn't count for much. It isn't an active, living faith.

Now think about Christmas. Rather than simply believing Christmas is true, insert yourself into the story. Think what it would have been like to believe the events would actually happen—before they happened. Imagine yourself as Joseph or Mary, both of whom were asked by God's messenger to do something extraordinary and quite unbelievable: to have faith in God that His only Son—the Savior who was coming to take away the sins of the world—was going to be born through them. Keep in mind that this was before anything had happened. They were asked to trust God before there was any physical evidence.

What if Mary and Joseph had believed God without acting

on their belief? What if they had not accepted the assignment God gave them? Because we know that God will always carry out His plans, it is certain He would have found two other people to get the job done.

Real faith—the kind that is so evident in the Christmas story—is more than knowledge about something. Real faith is about personally trusting God and believing that what He says is true, even before it happens. When we have that kind of faith, we have no choice but to respond to God's call on our lives the way Mary did:

> *"I am the Lord's servant. May everything you have said about me come true."*

LUKE 1:38

What is our faith worth if we don't trust God completely? When faced with a challenge or an opportunity to get on board with God, our natural tendency is to trust our own abilities and our own understanding of the situation. We don't want to act unless we're absolutely certain we can get the job done. But God will never use us if we take that approach. He wants us to trust Him with all our heart. He doesn't want us to depend on ourselves, but to seek His will in all we do.

If we do that, like Mary and Joseph and so many other great heroes of the faith have done, God promises to direct us in all we do—in the small stuff as well as the big—as He uses our work and our words for His glory.

- When you have faith, you have confident assurance that what you hope for is going to happen.

- When you have faith, you can believe in what you cannot see.

- There's no such thing as passive faith. True faith is *active*.

- When you combine belief and trust, you get faith.

- There is no limit to what God can do with the person who has faith.

But you, O Bethlehem. . .are only a
small village among all the people of Judah.
Yet a ruler of Israel will come from you, one whose
origins are from the distant past. And he will stand
to lead his flock with the LORD's strength, in the
majesty of the name of the LORD his God.
Then his people will live there undisturbed, for he
will be highly honored around the world.
And he will be the source of peace.

MICAH 5:2, 4–5

SIXTEEN

BETHLEHEM

What was God thinking? The event of the Messiah's birth was the perfect public relations opportunity. This was the celebrity birth of all eternity, and God could have caused media frenzy had He staged it differently. So why chose a tiny podunk town like Bethlehem for the big event?

If God had wanted worldwide attention for His Son's birth, He could have picked the then center of the known universe, Rome. It was the cultural, political, and commercial nucleus of the first-century world. If the Messiah's birth had happened in Rome, the news could have been quickly disseminated around the globe.

But even if God wanted to put a Jewish spin on the Messiah's birth, He could have arranged for it to take place in Jerusalem. In the religious realm, Jerusalem had been the Holy City throughout Hebrew history. While Jerusalem didn't have the cultural cache of Rome, it was a credible metropolis in its own right and certainly a worthy site for the birth of God's Son.

An argument could even be made for Jesus to be born in Nazareth, the residence of both Joseph and Mary. This would make sense, as Mary could have given birth with the aid of her mother and other relatives. East or west, home is best.

But Bethlehem? Why Bethlehem? It was a sleepy little village populated by sheepherders and farmers. Although it was only five miles south of Jerusalem, the two cities were worlds apart. There was nothing distinctive or special about it. Its only claim to fame was that it was the hometown of a young boy who killed a giant and then went on to assume the throne for all of Israel. But that had been about a thousand years ago. So village leaders were grasping at ancient history when they inscribed "Home of King David" on the WELCOME TO BETHLEHEM signs.

The answer to this quandary can be found in the writing of the ancient prophet Micah. About seven hundred years before the birth of Christ, God spoke through the prophet to declare that the Messiah would be born in the town of Bethlehem. This was a specific prophecy that could be fact-checked against anyone claiming to be the Messiah.

God frequently does things in ways that seem strange at the time. Often, His wisdom is revealed only when viewed after the fact. And so it is with the selection of Bethlehem as the Messiah's birthplace. Arranging for Jesus to be born in Rome or Jerusalem or even Nazareth would make sense to human understanding. But God wanted to prove that He was involved in every detail of this event.

Contemporary historians and statisticians can confirm it would have taken a miracle to have Mary's child born in Bethlehem when she and Joseph lived seventy miles to the north. Why would they venture on such a dangerous sojourn to Bethlehem, putting both Mary and the unborn child at great risk, when it was less a desirable place than Nazareth?

God knew all along that the Roman emperor, Caesar Augustus, would order everyone to travel to the hometown of their ancestors to register for a census. Since both Joseph and Mary were in the lineage of King David, they were required to travel to Bethlehem at the precise time Mary was expected to deliver her child. A coincidence? Hardly, if God knew the timing and had Micah announce the unlikely birth site hundreds of years in advance.

Can anyone really believe that Jesus was born in Bethlehem by happenstance or accident? No, and that is precisely why God orchestrated the circumstances in this fashion.

God works in the same way in your life. Just as He was intimately involved in the design details for the first Christmas, He is working in your life today.

. . .In the Small Stuff

- God's guidance of your life is more easily recognized in the rearview mirror. But God doesn't want you moving in reverse. He wants you to go faith forward.

- Be glad that God's accomplishments aren't limited by what you are able to comprehend.

- God delights in being involved in the small details of your life. You'll delight when you realize what He's done.

- Bethlehem rose out of obscurity when its population increased by One.

- The beauty of a miracle in your life is not primarily what it does for you but the attention that it brings to God.

She gave birth to her first child, a son. She wrapped
him snugly in strips of cloth
and laid him in a manger, because there was no
lodging available for them.

LUKE 2:7

SEVENTEEN

THE INN AND THE STABLE

One of the most reviled characters in the Bible is the innkeeper who rejected Mary and Joseph on the night Jesus was born. The young couple had journeyed from Nazareth to Bethlehem and was badly in need of a room for the night. Not only did they need shelter, they needed a warm and clean place for the "obviously pregnant" Mary to give birth. Unfortunately, the man who ran the village inn—often portrayed as a crude, heartless fellow—refused to provide a room, forcing a desperate Joseph to seek refuge for his wife and soon-to-be-born son in a stable full of animals.

Whenever this story is told, many develop a hatred for the innkeeper—putting him just one notch above Judas Iscariot, the renegade disciple who would betray Jesus thirty-three years later. To be sure, the story of the innkeeper makes for good drama. There's only one problem. This much-maligned fellow is never mentioned in the Bible. There's not even any evidence that such a character ever existed.

The other elements of this well-known story are true, although the Bible is light on the details of the full-to-capacity inn and the stable where Jesus was born. Yes, there was a village lodging place, but contrary to the embellished images you will often see in picture books, it probably wasn't a hotel with rooms, like some ancient Holiday Inn. More likely, as was the custom, it was a guest room in a private residence, or it could have been some sort of public shelter. Given Bethlehem's crowded conditions at the time of the census, it's not surprising that there were no rooms available that holy night. The only space for the young couple was a place reserved for animals.

Interestingly, the Bible never mentions animals, either. All it says is that Mary gave birth to a son, wrapped Him in strips of cloth (it was a sign of motherly care and affection to "swaddle" her baby in such a manner), and laid Him in a manger. The Bible doesn't tell us if sheep were bleating or cattle were lowing. It just says Mary put Jesus in a manger. However, since a manger was a feeding trough for animals, we can safely infer that Jesus was born with animals around.

As for the stable itself, it probably wasn't a quaint little barn like the ones you see in the picture books. In those days in Palestine, animals were often kept in a lower level room or stall attached to the living quarters of a private residence. Or it could have been a cave used as a shelter for animals, another common practice in that time.

Whatever the nature of the stable, it was a place suitable for animals, not the Savior of the world. Still, given the prophecies about the Messiah—"He was despised and rejected. . . . We turned our backs on him and looked the other way. He was despised, and we did not care" (Isaiah 53:3)—the setting of His birth was entirely appropriate. This humble beginning in a dark and dirty stable shows us the humility of Jesus, and it foreshadows the fact that He would attain glory through suffering.

Maybe the Jews expected their Messiah to be born in royal splendor, but this was never God's plan. This was never what Jesus had in mind.

*Though he was God, he did not think of equality with
God as something to cling to. Instead, he gave up his
divine privileges; he took the humble position of a slave
and was born as a human being.*

PHILIPPIANS 2:6–7

We should never limit God by our own expectations. He is
at work wherever He's needed in our dark and dirty world, and He's
looking for those who would willingly and faithfully follow Him.

What about the innkeeper—whether he actually existed or
not? Rather than despise him we should use him as an example, a
reminder to always have room for the Savior in our hearts and in
our lives.

. . .In the Small Stuff

- We don't do ourselves a favor by making the inn and the stable better places than they were.

- God delights in using humble things—and humble people—to carry out His plans.

- A good student of the Bible won't read more into the text than is already there.

- We should never limit God by our own expectations—because He is able to accomplish more than we could ever imagine.

- Jesus came to bring His light to the dark places in our world.

He who has not Christmas in his heart will never find it under a tree.

ROY L. SMITH

EIGHTEEN

THE CHRISTMAS TREE

You could spend your lifetime reading and rereading the Bible's Christmas story, and you'll never find mention of a Christmas tree. Maybe, since the birth of Jesus marked the very first Christmas, there were no preexisting Christmas customs and traditions for Mary and Joseph to follow. More likely, there's no mention of Christmas trees near the manger because there were no evergreen fir trees in the area around Bethlehem. (There were olive and fig trees in the neighborhood, but they don't have a nice conical shape—and no obvious place to put the decorative star or angel on top.)

Any book discussing the small stuff of Christmas should include some mention of Christmas trees, even if they aren't mentioned in the Bible. Accordingly, this is our chapter for doing so.

Who could have guessed that the Christmas tree would become so controversial for Christians? The current debate in some Christian circles—only Christians argue about these kinds of things—is whether the Christmas tree is a pagan emblem that should be exorcised from our Christmas celebrations. (One radical group even suggests that Christians should disdain Christmas itself since it's merely a sanitized version of a pagan winter holiday—as they believe the true date of Jesus' birth was probably in the spring.)

Most rational people don't extract ancient Druid symbolism from a Christmas tree. They just think it's a nice holiday decoration that originated in the time of Queen Victoria and Prince Albert in the 1800s. We know of no families that worship their trees. (Most can't even remember to add water to the tree stand.)

We can't overlook the fact that the apostle Paul said Christians could eat day-old meat that had been offered to idols and was being sold at a discount; those first-century Christians weren't engaging in pagan idol worship, just seeking a bargain. In the same way, the fact that some ancient pagan cultures used trees as idols shouldn't prohibit the use of trees as twenty-first-century Christmas decorations; dead wood with tinsel isn't an idol unless you worship it.

Apparently some Christians—being sensitive to the commercialization of Christmas—have tried to implant (no pun intended) religious significance into the Christmas tree to justify its prominent place in their family room during the month of December. They point out that the baby Jesus was laid in a manger *made out of wood*; He spent his first night on earth in a stable *made out of wood*; and He subsequently died on a cross *made out of wood*. Since a Christmas tree is *made out of wood*, it serves to remind us of Jesus in these ways. (This rationale, unfortunately, rules out the use of artificial trees made of plastic and particularly those retro aluminum trees.) Some who rely on this Christmas tree justification go a step further by analogizing the decorative ornaments to the "fruit of the Spirit" of Galatians 5:22–23.

But maybe these strained analogies aren't necessary. The fact that there is no direct spiritual significance to a Christmas tree does not detract from its splendor and sentimental significance. If a decorated tree brings joy and beauty into your home, we're sure God is pleased with it.

The Christmas tree is not the real issue. The subtext to the debate is how you celebrate Christmas. Do you make it a holy day with Christ at the center? Or is Christmas just an excuse for overindulgence of a commercialized nature? If Christ is the heart of your celebration, then the Christmas tree can be a lovely part of your decorating scheme. But if you've left Jesus out of the big picture, you aren't really celebrating a Christ-centered Christmas anyway—and it's entirely irrelevant whether your family room is occupied by a tastefully decorated tree or a dancing Satns in an aloha shirt.

- The best Christmas tree is the one surrounded by your friends and family.

- When your children are grown, they'll forget what gifts you gave them—but they'll remember those meaningful Christmas traditions you celebrated.

- Those who argue for strict authenticity in the celebration of Christmas might try spending the holiday as homeless outcasts giving birth in a barn.

- Decorations shouldn't be necessary to keep your thoughts on Jesus—but if they help, use them.

- God is more concerned about His place in your heart than about the decorations in your home.

Joy to the world, the Lord is come!
Let earth receive her King;
Let every heart prepare Him room,
And Heaven and nature sing.

ISAAC WATTS

NINETEEN

PREPARE HIM ROOM

Every Christmas it's the same. You remember what it was like last year when you ran yourself ragged trying to get everything done. There were dinners to plan; programs to attend; parades and bowl games to watch; friends to have over; relatives to visit; presents to buy, wrap, open, and return. It's not like you set a goal to be busy. It just ended up that way.

But when the season passed, you felt exhausted and ashamed that you had missed the real meaning of Christmas—so this year you decided that things would be different. You're not going to get caught up in the frenzy. . .but the squeeze is already beginning. Your calendar is starting to fill up, your lists are lengthening. It's all good, right? It's all important.

So why do you feel like there's something missing? Probably because something really is missing. Or should we say *someone* is missing. Someone named Jesus.

We're not saying that you've intentionally left Jesus out of Christmas. It's just happening, the way it does every year. Because of everything else you've crammed into your life during this sacred season, you literally have no room. . . .

No room in your schedule
No room for quiet and reflection
No room for solitude
No room in your resources
No room for Jesus

On that first Christmas night there was no room for Jesus

in the village inn. Now, during this Christmas season, once again there is no room. Because you haven't left any room in your schedule, your thoughts, your resources, and your heart, there's no room for the One who is the reason for the season. At the very time of year that should belong to Him, you're letting Jesus know that He doesn't belong.

It's not the way you want it. We know that, because we've been right where you are—many times. It's embarrassing. It's discouraging. But you know what? It doesn't have to be this way. We can do better. You can do better. But how?

As the Christmas carol "Joy to the World" suggests, giving Jesus room in our schedules, our thoughts, our resources, and our hearts doesn't happen on its own. It takes thoughtful preparation. It takes careful planning. It takes intentional thinking. It takes opening our hearts. In short, it takes our best efforts to move Jesus from the fringes to the center of our lives.

Maybe the secret to our preparing Him room lies in the way we view Jesus. If we see Him in that manger year after year, we're going to keep thinking of Him as a baby. But we can't leave Jesus there, all wrapped up in that little feeding trough. We need to unwrap Him and give Him the room He deserves by letting Him grow in our lives.

. . .In the Small Stuff

- No room in your schedule means no opportunity for Jesus to do something surprising in your life.

- No room for quiet and reflection means no chance for you to hear God's still, small voice in your thoughts.

- No room for solitude means no place for you to be alone with God.

- No room in your resources means no possibility that you will enjoy the blessing of giving to God's work.

- No room for Jesus means no way for you to truly appreciate Christmas.

I dreamed it was Christmas Eve,
and while waiting for a green light
I noticed the manger scene on the church lawn.
It's all so overwhelming,
this Christmas business, I thought.
The shopping and singing and partying
and gift wrapping and Santa Claus and Jesus.
I feel wonderful then guilty
then joyful then confused. *God help me,* I thought.
And the light changed, and the
baby in the manger smiled.

JOE HICKMAN

TWENTY

THE BIRTH OF JESUS

Our mental pictures of the night of Christ's birth are probably unrealistic. Most likely, we're guilty of imagining the event as a bit too pristine. With the stained-glass images of the manger scene, and the little halo above the baby Jesus' head in those Renaissance paintings, we know that the Son of God was there in the stable. But we tend to picture Him as God in a pint-sized human package. We forget that baby Jesus was equally human, with all the complications that accompany birth.

To fully understand the fact that Jesus was both God and Man, we need to accurately envision what happened in the stable that first Christmas night. Maybe the events began earlier in the afternoon with Mary doubled over in pain, her contractions increasing in frequency. There was no place for her to lie down, because she and Joseph were still on the hunt for lodging. She couldn't ride comfortably on the donkey, and she couldn't walk without severe distress. She was miserable.

Joseph wasn't in pain, but he was probably panicked. He was doing a poor job of providing and protecting when Mary most needed his help. Perhaps he was frantic to find a safe place for her, fearing that she might injure herself or the baby if she wasn't soon settled.

As afternoon became evening, Mary's contractions grew relentless, her cries of pain perhaps so loud that she could have been heard by the shepherds outside of town—if they hadn't been distracted by the singing of the angelic hosts. Joseph, who had probably only been involved in his own birth, was useless as a midwife. All he could manage to do was to wipe the sweat from Mary's forehead and pray that this baby would make a quick entrance.

Our disinfected view of the birth of Christ would be shattered if we had seen the real event. It was messy and unsanitary.

The hay was soaked in blood. The animals were probably frightened by Mary's cries, jumping about and kicking up dust. In the midst of this chaos, the baby Jesus was born, not at all plump and adorable. He was howling and distressed from the difficult delivery. Joseph would have tried to wash Mary and the infant the best he could, but without clean water available, he probably had to brush away scum from the top of the trough to soak some rags in the infested water of the stable. It was not a pretty sight.

But God the Father loved you so much He was willing to let His Son endure this experience. Sure, God could have made things easier. But that was never the deal with Christ's life on earth. Yes, Jesus was both God and man, but He never used His supernatural God powers to make His human life easier. He felt pain at His birth; and He probably got hurt playing as a child. He might have been embarrassed and humiliated by other kids who taunted and ostracized Him for being conceived out of wedlock. And we know that as an adult He was often the target of slander and unwarranted accusations, leading up to His torture and crucifixion. He lived a human life, just as you and I have done, but with more severity. He endured all the pain and difficulty of humanity; none of it was minimized the least little bit by His deity.

That is both the good news and the bad news. It was bad news for Christ but good news for us. It means we have a Savior who knows what we are going through. We have a God who knows about human pain and sorrow and suffering. We have a God who can comfort us because He can sympathize with us. That is a precious gift that we often overlook when we celebrate Christmas.

- Christ endured pain so that you might experience peace.

- The Old Testament patriarchs had the privilege of knowing God—but Mary had the higher honor of holding Him.

- The composer who wrote the lyrics to "Silent Night" wasn't standing outside the stable.

- Our love for God will grow in direct proportion to our understanding of the pain He suffered for us.

- Any pain or sorrow you endure has already been experienced by God.

"Look! The virgin will conceive a child!
She will give birth to a son
and will call him Immanuel
(which means 'God is with us')."

ISAIAH 7:14

TWENTY-ONE

GOD WITH US

One of the most important—if not *the* most important—question anyone can ask is this: "How does God relate to the world?" If you were to ask that question in a random group of people, say at a mall or a public gathering of some kind, you would get all kinds of answers.

Some would say that God created the world, then withdrew—and isn't all that interested in what's going on. Others would say that God may have been powerful enough to make everything, but He certainly isn't strong enough to stop all the suffering and evil in the world. Still others would say that the question is irrelevant, because there's really no God anyway although it's okay to believe in some sort of "cosmic power" if it helps you sleep at night.

If by chance there was someone in the crowd who really understood what the Bible says about God, and if this person was confident enough to give an answer that isn't all that popular these days, here's what you would hear: Jesus Christ.

Jesus is both the *Christian* answer and also the *Christmas* answer to the question, "How does God relate to the world?", because Jesus is God in human form. He is "the visible image of the invisible God" (Colossians 1:15). The technical term for the process of God taking on human form is *incarnation*, which comes from a Latin word meaning "taking" or "being flesh". In the Bible the concept of the incarnation is best expressed in John 1:14: "So the Word became human and made his home among us."

This verse, where Jesus is referred to as the living Word of God, also conveys the idea that God became a human so He could come to earth and *live among us*. That's the essence of the name given to Jesus by the prophet Isaiah: *Immanuel*, which means "God with us." What powerful words! John MacArthur has said, "If we condense all the truths of Christmas into only three words, these would be the words."

Imagine the Creator of the universe taking on human form—the form of a *baby*—so that He could be with us! It's not that we're all that great to be around. We make mistakes and say the wrong things. Some of us say nasty things about God, while others prefer to think that He doesn't exist. As humans, we can be an unsavory bunch, yet the all-powerful, all-knowing, completely holy and faithful Creator of the universe willingly came in the form of a frail baby to hang out with us and show us a better way to live.

Because of Jesus, we know that God is with us. We also know that God loves us and that God is for us. Even more, because Jesus is God, we have someone who can save us—because He lived a perfect life and became the perfect sacrifice for our sins.

Because Jesus is human, He can identify with our weaknesses. We don't have to worry that God is detached from our world, not caring about us. He knows what we are going through, and He is able to help us in our distress.

. . .In the Small Stuff

- If God is with you, you are never alone.

- If God is for you, nothing can be against you.

- Because God is both with you and for you, anything He has done for anyone, He can do for you.

- Jesus may not be living on earth right now, but He is living—and wants a personal relationship with you.

- Jesus is the ultimate expression of God's love.

Suddenly, the angel was joined by a vast
host of others—the armies of heaven—
praising God and saying,
"Glory to God in highest heaven,
and peace on earth to those with
whom God is pleased."

TWENTY-TWO

ANGELS

A little snippet of the Christmas story is told in the Gospel of Matthew, but the Bible's longest narrative of Christmas events is found chapters 1 and 2 of Luke's Gospel. Not surprisingly, the writer of the Gospel of Luke was a guy named Luke. He was a Gentile Christian—a Greek by nationality—who was a friend and traveling partner of the apostle Paul.

When he wasn't researching and writing the Gospel of Luke and the book of Acts, Luke earned his living as a physician.

With medical training in his background, he was naturally curious about details and wanted to get the facts correct. While he wasn't an eyewitness to Christ's birth, Bible scholars believe he personally interviewed Mary and searched for other first-hand accounts of that special night.

With his scientific background, Luke knew how to research a topic from all angles. So it's not surprising that he reports impressions from an earthly perspective—those of Mary and Joseph and the shepherds. But Luke went a step further, also reporting impressions of the first Christmas from a heavenly perspective. The human reaction was wonder and amazement, but the response of the angelic hosts was sheer joy and celebration.

The songs of praise sung by those armies of angels must have penetrated the skies for miles around. The shepherds probably covered their ears for protection from the ear-splitting volume. Had the angels hovered over a city rather than the barren Judean hillsides, residents would undoubtedly have been awakened from their sleep by the celestial anthems.

But the angelic songfest wasn't God's promotional hype to publicize the birth of His Son to everyone. He wanted to limit the announcement to a small group of shepherds, and that message was adequately handled by a single angel. (Those shepherds were "terrified" by the appearance of one angel—they were sorely impressed and received the message loud and clear. God didn't need to add angel armies to make an impact on them.)

So why all the angelic hoopla? The angels couldn't help themselves. Maybe they weren't scheduled into the program as much as they were compelled to break out in spontaneous celebration.

The whole story of the Messiah's birth took people by surprise. Mary and Joseph had only had nine months to mentally prepare for it. News of the birth totally shocked the shepherds. It's understandable that the human reactions were heavily influenced by considerable confusion. But not with the angels. They knew exactly what was happening, and their celebration included a release of pent-up anticipation. They couldn't help themselves. They were exploding with excitement.

Consider that the angels probably knew of God's plan for saving the human race long before the world was created. At least from the time of Adam and Eve, the angels knew God was eventually going to send His Son to earth to be the sacrificial offering for the sins of mankind. Their comprehension of the significance of this event was much deeper and more exhaustive than the limited understanding of Mary and Joseph. The angels knew the big picture. They had been waiting thousands of years for this event to take place. They were excited that God's plan was coming to fruition; they were celebrating the enormity of Christ's love to make such a tremendous sacrifice; and they were overjoyed that all of humanity could receive the eternal benefit of what was occurring in a little barnyard lean-to in Bethlehem.

What is *your* excitement level when you hear the Christmas story? You enjoy an enviable vantage point similar to that of the angels: You don't suffer the limited perspective and understanding of Mary, Joseph, and the shepherds. You get the big picture. You know the significance of what happened.

Considering what God accomplished that night in Bethlehem, we should explode with praise—even if our voices aren't quite as melodious as the angel choir.

- The angels were the first choir to perform at a Christmas Eve service.

- You don't have to sing like an angel, but the Christmas season should at least put a song in your heart.

- The next time you see the thrill in a child's eyes on Christmas morning, imagine the angels' excitement at seeing God present the gift of His Son to humanity.

- What gift do you get for the human race that has nothing? The Son of God, who has everything they need.

- The level of your excitement about the Christmas story may indicate the degree of your love for God.

It is Christmas in the heart that
puts Christmas in the air.

W. T. ELLIS

TWENTY-THREE

CHRISTMAS CAROLS

Many people worry that our public places—schools, town squares, government buildings, and the like—are locking Christ out of Christmas. We suppose they have a point. What used to be a "Christmas vacation" in our public schools is now a "holiday break." Student performers in the "Winter Program" (it used to be called a "Christmas Program") are generally forbidden to sing "sacred" Christmas carols. Only songs about snowmen, chestnuts, and Santa Claus will do. And you would be hard-pressed to find a nativity scene in front of a courthouse.

Such developments may discourage those of us who grew up with Christmas carols and crèches all around, but does the loss of these traditions from the public square truly hinder our celebration of Christmas? Do we really need a plastic nativity scene on the side of the road to remind us that Christ was born?

Okay, so maybe you're thinking of those who don't grasp the true meaning of Christmas. Don't they need the reminders? Indeed they do, but before you organize a boycott of your child's grade school because they won't let her sing "Away in a Manger" in the Winter Program, think about this: The true meaning and message of Christmas is being broadcast in public places like never before, thanks to the recent phenomenon of the "All Christmas Music—All the Time" programming found on hundreds of radio stations across the country.

Back when Christmas carols were still being sung in the public schools, you rarely heard radio stations playing Christmas music except on December 24 and 25. And even then it was mixed in with their regular fare. But with the demise of Christmas carol performances in our schools has come the rise of Christmas carol broadcasts on our radio stations (stations, we might add, that would otherwise never consider playing a song about Jesus).

Make no mistake about it: Those hundreds of radio-station owners aren't playing Christmas carols because they love Jesus (although some of them might). No, the thing that drives these media moguls is commerce, pure and simple. What they find is that if they program Christmas music twenty-four hours a day for the entire Christmas season, their ratings go up—sometimes all the way to number one—and, consequently, so does their revenue. Don't be upset that stations are using Christmas carols for their own gain. The truth is, God is using those radio stations for His gain.

Oh sure, there are plenty of corny and sentimental secular Christmas songs being played along with the sacred carols, but so what? That's exactly the way God wants it. His message of hope and love and forgiveness—for a world crying out for all three—is best seen against the darkness, like a sparkling diamond displayed on a black velvet background.

So if you feel angry that your kids can't perform "Hark! The Herald Angels Sing" in school, thank God that it's being heard by millions through radios in cars, homes, and yes, even in public places. And be thankful that the true meaning and message of Christmas comes through loud and clear in carols like this one that proclaim the true and timeless message of Christmas:

Hark! the herald angels sing,
"Glory to the newborn King;
Peace on earth, and mercy mild,
God and sinners reconciled!"
Joyful, all ye nations rise,
Join the triumph of the skies;
With th' angelic host proclaim,
"Christ is born in Bethlehem."

Hark! the herald angels sing,
"Glory to the newborn King!"

Hail the heav'nly Prince of Peace!
Hail the Sun of Righteousness!
Light and life to all He brings,
Ris'n with healing in His wings.
Mild He lays His glory by,
Born that man no more may die.
Born to raise the sons of earth,
Born to give them second birth.

Hark! the herald angels sing,
"Glory to the newborn King!"

- God can and will use any means possible to proclaim His message of hope and love and forgiveness.

- There's a reason why Christmas carols never go out of style: Their message is timeless.

- Since your children aren't learning Christmas carols in school, intentionally sing them at home.

- Don't be upset when culture prohibits the sights and sounds of Christmas in public. Instead, do all you can to proclaim the meaning of Christmas personally.

- Whatever your vocal ability, Christmas carols sound better when sung from the heart.

That night there were shepherds staying in the fields nearby, guarding their flocks of sheep. Suddenly, an angel of the Lord appeared among them,and the radiance of the Lord's glory surrounded them. They were terrified, but the angel reassured them. "Don't be afraid!" he said. "I bring you good news that will bring great joy to all people. The Savior—yes, the Messiah, the Lord—has been born today in Bethlehem, the city of David!" When the angels had returned to heaven, the shepherds said to each other, "Let's go to Bethlehem! Let's see this thing that has happened,which the Lord has told us about." They hurried to the village and found Mary and Joseph. And there was the baby, lying in the manger. After seeing him, the shepherds told everyone what had happened and what the angel had said to them about this child. All who heard the shepherds' story were astonished.

LUKE 2:8–12, 15–1

TWENTY-FOUR

SHEPHERDS

The beauty of the Christmas story is its simplicity—which is wrapped around intricate theology. The angel's encounter with the shepherds that first Christmas night reveals the dual aspects of commonplace humanity and majestic deity.

On the scale of occupational excitement, shepherding is probably low on the list. Oh sure, there's the occasional shooing-away of a predatory animal, but an accurate fling with a sling can remedy that rather quickly. For the most part, shepherds experience the serenity of the landscape while listening to the rhythmic *baas* of the sheep herd. Such a job might seem nice in the abstract, but after a couple decades of living with farm animals, one might be inclined to wish for a different career. On the social scale, shepherds were not highly esteemed for their contributions.

In this cultural context, God chose to make the greatest announcement of all time to those who were the least sophisticated. The angel didn't proclaim Jesus' birth in the temple courtyard in Jerusalem; he didn't wake the super-religious Pharisees with his declaration; and he totally bypassed the upper-class Sadducees. Instead, he went to the working-class shepherds. By doing so, the angel emphasized the utter simplicity of God's message: No snooty education or self-indulgent social status was required to understand that the Messiah had arrived. And that's why the angel declared the announcement "good news" for "all people."

So the shepherds, who had the least credibility to speak about religious issues, were the ones who brought God's message to the masses. They got the buzz started by telling everyone they could find. Ordinarily, a shepherd spouting off about theological matters might have landed himself in a padded stable pending psychiatric testing. But there was something sincere and believable about the testimony of these ragtag herders. Instead of natural skepticism, astonishment filled those who heard their message.

The shepherds were unlikely candidates for carrying such news, but they were trustworthy guys. They probably weren't shrewd enough to pull off a scam, and, unlike the Pharisees and Sadducees who often acted fraudulently from ulterior motives, they would have no motivation for doing so. The simplicity of it all made the report believable.

There was an even deeper theological message in the angel's news flash that the shepherds overlooked. Since the Jews had been waiting centuries for their Messiah, they assumed they had proprietary ownership of Him. He was "their guy" and the changes He would institute would be for the exclusive benefit of Jews. But all Jews—shepherds, priests, and scholars alike—were clueless to one major reality: When the angel said this was "good news that will bring great joy to all people," the angel really meant *all people*—Gentiles as well as Jews. Hence the theological complexity.

The "all people" announced by the angel to the shepherds includes you. The Messiah was born a Jew as God had promised, and He came to bring salvation and freedom to the Jews as God had promised. But His earthly visit was a rescue mission for the rest of humanity, as well.

The "good news" told to the shepherds was deceptively simple. Yes, the Messiah had arrived; that message was simple enough. But the concept that the Messiah was a Savior for all people was mind boggling. For the first time the message of God's reconciliation extended to *everyone*, regardless of race or ethnicity, social background or breeding, sordid backgrounds or past failures.

The simple message the shepherds understood was good enough for them—but the rest of us can be thankful for the more complex meaning.

- God delights in using people we consider less deserving than ourselves.

- The good news of the Messiah is so simple you have no excuse for not sharing it.

- If someone is skeptical about the message of the Messiah, give the advice the angel gave the shepherds: "Check it out for yourself."

- When the shepherds returned to work, they were still praising God for what they had seen and heard. Why do we stop praising God for what we've seen and heard by the time we get to our car in the church parking lot?

- The "good news that will bring great joy to all people," given by the angel to the shepherds, is still applicable today.

"I bring you good news that will
bring great joy to all people."

LUKE 2:10

TWENTY–FIVE

JOY

Angels are often referred to as "God's messengers" because that's what they do: They carry God's message to us humans. They aren't ordinary messengers, of course, and whenever we read about their messages and the method of delivery, we can only begin to imagine what it was like to really be "touched by an angel."

When the angel brought word of Jesus' birth to the shepherds, the poor guys were scared out of their tunics. The Bible simply says they were "terrified," primarily due to the incredible "radiance of the Lord's glory" that surrounded the angelic being.

Not one to let the shepherds grovel in fear, the angel reassured them by saying, "Don't be afraid! I bring you good news that will bring great joy to all people." After a celestial choir concert, the shepherds, filled with the joy of the Lord, ran to see "this thing that has happened, which the Lord has told us about." And then they told everyone who would listen (and, we suspect, some who would not) the good news of what they had just seen.

Thus began the story of Jesus on earth. Thirty-three years later, after He had lived His remarkable life, after He was crucified and resurrected, the angel appeared again (we like to think it was the same angel, perhaps Gabriel, one of God's favorites), surrounded by the Lord's glory as before. Once again, he inspired fear among the mortals, this time two women. And as he had done with the shepherds, the angel reassured them by saying, "Don't be afraid! I know you are looking for Jesus, who was crucified. He isn't here! He is risen from the dead, just as he said would happen" (Matthew 28:5–6). As the women left the angel and the empty tomb, they ran to tell others the good news of what they had seen. The Bible says, "They were very frightened but also filled with great joy" (Matthew 28:8).

Don't you find it interesting that in both of these accounts there are four elements:

- An angel, surrounded by God's glory, appeared to ordinary people;

- The people, due to the angel's glorious appearance, reacted with great fear;

- After being told they had nothing to be afraid of, the people were filled with great joy; and

- They couldn't wait to tell others what they had seen.

Like bookends on the earthly life of Christ, these parallel accounts tell us exactly *how* and *why* God has given us His joy. The *how* is pretty easy to see. God gave us His joy when He sent Jesus to be born. And then He gave us His joy again when He raised Jesus from the dead.

More perplexing is the *why*. Why would God share His joy with those who had turned their backs on Him? For the answer, you have to go back to God's character. It is in the nature of God to love us and share Himself with us, and that includes His joy. Jesus is the absolute fullest expression of God's joy, and one of the reasons He came was to give us lives full of joy (John 10:10). When we obey Jesus and immerse ourselves in His love, He guarantees that our lives will be filled with joy. Jesus said, "Yes, your joy will overflow!" (John 15:11).

But God also gives us joy because that gives *Him* joy. As God's joy takes root in us, as we enjoy Him and give Him glory, the Bible says He rejoices in us with great gladness (Zephaniah 3:17).

Now there's a reason to soak up all that Christmas has to offer. It's full of joy. . .God's joy. As we celebrate God's love for us and respond to Him in joy, the reason for the season will become incredibly meaningful for us—in the small stuff as well as the big.

. . .In the Small Stuff

- Happiness is temporary; joy is everlasting.

- If you've lost your joy, maybe it's time you found Jesus.

- You will never be joyful unless you are full of joy.

- By its very nature, joy overflows. That's why it's impossible to keep joy to yourself.

- Just as the darkest hour comes before dawn, your joy will often follow a time of deep sadness.

Purify me from my sins, and I will be clean;
wash me, and I will be whiter than snow.

PSALM 51:7

TWENTY-SIX

SNOW

Think of any epic biblical movie you've seen. Whether you go back to the 1956 classic *The Ten Commandments*, with Charlton Heston as Moses in a pasted-on beard, or something more contemporary like Mel Gibson's *The Passion of the Christ*, one thing is for sure: There's not a lot of snow in the scenery. Bible territory is known for heat and dust, but let's face it—snow isn't an image that comes to mind when you picture that first Christmas night (or, for that matter, any other scene from the pages of the Bible).

Snow was rare, but not an unknown climatological concept to the Jews of the Old Testament. The white stuff is even occasionally mentioned in the Bible as a symbol of refreshment. While many people may have gone a lifetime without personally experiencing snow, they could have seen it in the distance. Mt. Hermon, elevation 9,100 feet above sea level, is on the northern boundary of the territory known as the Promised Land. Snowfall on Mt. Hermon was regular, and sometimes heavy. From the torturously hot plains of Galilee, the snow-capped Mt. Hermon could be seen by the Israelites. To them, snow represented physical and spiritual refreshment they could hope for and dream about. It often carried a connotation of something to be looked forward to.

Snow is used in another biblical analogy, this one relating to its color rather than its temperature. The psalmist compares the untainted whiteness of new-fallen snow with purity—the way God sees us after He's forgiven our sins. Sin is characterized by darkness, but the condition of our hearts after God's forgiveness is "whiter than snow."

For many people, those who live in heavy-snow regions,

the white stuff is something to be shoveled, a miserable and treacherous nuisance. Not everyone can relate to the biblical imagery of snow as anticipated refreshment. But all of us carry the baggage of past acts that shame us; we have regret and guilt for things we've done or things we should have done but didn't. So the biblical metaphor of the purity of snow resonates with us, because we all want to be set free from our private shame. We all want our conscience to be "whiter than snow."

As you seek to keep Christ at the center of your Christmas, use the appearance of snow scenes to remind you of Him. You're guaranteed to see lots of snow during the Christmas season. If you live in certain climates, you'll see it out the window. You'll find it on Christmas cards. And you'll see it depicted in the displays in store windows. When you actually look for it, you'll see it everywhere. And when you do, remember that biblical reference: Your sins can be forgiven, and God will see the condition of your heart as pure as the new-fallen snow.

This freedom doesn't occur automatically. And it certainly doesn't happen by jolly St. Nicholas putting his finger alongside his nose. It comes through your belief that the infant in the manger that first Christmas was the Savior of the world. It happens when we choose to put Christ first in our lives, not just at Christmastime, but always.

- Living life with a heart "whiter than snow" is the true celebration of Christmas.

- Forgiveness that makes your heart "whiter than snow" also gives you a warm feeling inside.

- God doesn't forgive until we confess.

- God's gift for you is His unconditional love and forgiveness. He left it for you—wrapped and lying in a manger.

- Christmas is rushed if you cram it all into one month. Christmas is best enjoyed throughout the entire year.

Jesus was born in Bethlehem in Judea,
during the reign of King Herod.
About that time some wise men from eastern lands
arrived in Jerusalem, asking,
"Where is the newborn king of the Jews?
We saw his star as it rose,
and we have come to worship him."

MATTHEW 2:1–2

TWENTY-SEVEN

THE WISE MEN

A common saying at Christmastime makes an important statement: "Wise men still seek Him." The implication is that if you are wise, you will seek Jesus, just like the wise men—or *magi* as they are sometimes called—followed the star until they found "the newborn king of the Jews."

The story of the wise men, found only in the Gospel of Matthew, offers several lessons on what it means to truly seek Jesus today. Watch what these first-century astrologers did, and how God used them for His glory:

The wise men were looking. At first glance, it appears these men of high position woke up one day, saw a bright star, and decided to follow it. But there's much more to the story than that. Though the Bible doesn't say much about the wise men, history tells us that they probably came from a region near the site of ancient Babylon, where reading the stars and signs was serious business. It's possible the wise men had studied the Old Testament, left by Jewish exiles centuries earlier. They might have read the prophecy, "A star will rise from Jacob" (Numbers 24:17). Armed with their knowledge of the scriptures, they were probably looking for some indication that the prophecy was true.

God sent them a sign. A lot of people want God to send them a sign. "If you're really out there, God, show me!" The problem is that people really aren't looking for God. They want God to look for them. Not so the wise men. They were earnestly looking, so God responded by sending them a sign—a star. Do you know that God would love to send you a sign? All you have to do is look for Him. The Bible says that God "rewards those who sincerely seek him" (Hebrews 11:6).

The wise men committed to a journey. Seeking God takes commitment. Just because God gives you a sign doesn't mean your job is done. You need to embark on a spiritual journey. You have to get out of your comfort zone and do what it takes to truly find God. That's what the wise men did. They set aside their routine, made the commitment to follow God's leading, and traveled a great distance to find the Messiah.

The wise men brought gifts. The wise men didn't begin their journey empty-handed. They brought gifts that honored Jesus. The gold was a gift fit for a king; the frankincense was a fragrance signifying deity; and the myrrh was a spice used to anoint a body for burial. The wise men probably didn't realize the true significance of their gifts, but God did. He knew that the King of Kings and Lord of Lords would one day lay down His life for all people. God used the wise men's gifts for His glory.

The wise men listened to God's voice. The sign God gave the wise men led them to Jesus, but God wasn't done. He spoke to them in a dream and told them to return home another way so

King Herod wouldn't know where Jesus was. God still speaks today—through a still, small voice speaking through His Word, both written and living. "My sheep listen to my voice," said Jesus. "I know them, and they follow me" (John 10:27).

There's one final aspect to the wise men's story that shows us how God uses those who are obedient to Him. After the wise men returned to their homeland, God spoke to Joseph through an angel and told him that because Herod intended to kill Jesus, Joseph and Mary needed to flee to Egypt with their precious child. Historians tell us that in order to raise money for the trip, it's quite possible Joseph sold the gifts the wise men had given.

How amazing—and how comforting—to know that God always sees the big picture. He always provides for those He loves, using whatever gifts we give Him for our own benefit and His glory.

. . .In the Small Stuff

- If you're waiting for God to send you a sign, you've probably missed the ones He already sent.

- If you haven't seen a sign from God in a while, maybe you haven't been seeking Him.

- God will never use your gifts if you haven't given them to Him.

- God always knows the significance of our gifts, even if we don't.

- The extent of your ministry for Christ will be determined by the depth of your obedience to Him.

The star they had seen in the east
guided them to Bethlehem.
It went ahead of them and stopped
over the place where the child was.
When they saw the star, they were filled with joy!

MATTHEW 2:9–10

TWENTY-EIGHT

THE STAR

In the hierarchy of Christmas ornaments, the position of honor goes to the one placed at the top of the tree. In most households, this distinction belongs to. . .drum roll, please. . ."the star." ("The angel" comes in a distant second as the most popular tree-topper, and there are no serious contenders after that.)

How did the star earn such a privileged position in Christmas decorating schemes? After all, in the historical account of the first Christmas, the star doesn't have lead billing. It's not mentioned in the Christmas account as reported in Luke's Gospel;

you'll only find it mentioned in the book of Matthew—and even there it gets only a brief reference in four verses (chapter 2, verses 2, 7, 9, and 10).

What do we know—or *not* know—about this famous star?

- It was noticed by the wise men who lived far away in the East. But the shepherds in the hills outside Bethlehem apparently didn't see it. (They saw angels but had to run around the back alleys of Bethlehem seeking a makeshift delivery room in a stable.) Apparently, there was no huge star suspended a few feet above the stable as is often depicted in paintings and in that nativity scene your kid made out of Popsicle sticks.

- The star announced and publicized the birth of the Savior to those wise men, and based on their study of the Old Testament, they journeyed to Jerusalem to make further inquiry. After consultation with the sages in King Herod's court, it was determined that Bethlehem would be the Messiah's birthplace according to the ancient prophets. As soon as the wise men resumed their trek, now headed toward Bethlehem, the star appeared to them again. It "went ahead of them" on the way to Bethlehem. Since quite awhile had passed between the initial appearance of the star and the wise men's journey to Jerusalem, Jesus and his parents were no longer in the stable. They were most likely settled into some temporary housing. The star must have had accurate "MapQuesting" capabilities, because the wise men didn't have to knock on every door in the neighborhood. The star actually "stopped over the place where the child was."

Astronomers have long speculated about the nature of the star. Was that first sighting an unidentified comet? Maybe it was the alignment of Jupiter, Saturn, and Mars that occurred in 6 BC. Or maybe there were two stars: The first could have been an anomaly in the constellations, noticed by astronomers as a special occurrence, which would have meaning to anyone studying the scriptures and looking for hints as to the arrival of the Messiah. The second could have been a star that, with pinpoint accuracy, could identify a specific house in GPS-like fashion, but was only visible to the wise men—so as not to reveal the baby's location to King Herod.

The Bible is not a science textbook. For example, it refers

to God as a shepherd, revealing details about His character—but it doesn't tell us how to clone a sheep. So the lack of a scientific explanation of the star of Bethlehem should cause us no concern.

In nontechnical and nontheoretical language, the Bible tells it like it happened: God used a star in the sky to proclaim to the wise men that the Messiah had arrived. Later, God used a star to miraculously lead the wise men to the very house in which Mary, Joseph, and the baby Jesus were living. When viewed in this context, the star is simply one of many circumstances that illustrate God's intricate plan.

And maybe that's what the star on your tree should represent: something to draw your attention to God's involvement in Christmas. He invented the holiday, you know.

- Christ was the real star of Christmas—and, eventually, He ended up on top of a tree.

- The star of Bethlehem was a one-time event. So was Christmas. Every year since we've just celebrated an anniversary.

- The wise men were first attracted by the star. Later, they worshiped the child who came to be the Light of the World.

- The wise men looked for the Messiah's announcement in the sky. You'll find it easier simply to read the New Testament.

- God isn't interested in playing hide-and-seek. He wants you to find Him. And He will make Himself obvious if you just start looking.

I'll be home for Christmas. . . .

JAMES GANNON

TWENTY-NINE

HOME FOR CHRISTMAS

 F ew words better capture the emotion and the attraction of Christmas than *home*. The simple lyrics from the song, "I'll Be Home for Christmas"—originally written from the perspective of World War II soldiers—instantly inspire longing for that place in our memories (or in our dreams) where the warmth of family and the joys of the year's most wonderful time come together.

The reason home has such universal appeal is simple. Home is the primary place where we are known and loved. The classic

Cheers bar, "where everybody knows your name," is at best in third place. Even the workplace, where many people spend more time than anywhere else, is a distant second. There's only one place that holds the top spot in our hearts, and that's home. There are no sweeter words than those you utter at the end of a long journey, especially at Christmastime: "I'm finally home."

Yet for all its warmth and familiarity, there can be something disconcerting about home—and it's not just the heated discussions that sometimes erupt, or the cruel words that occasionally slip out not long after we arrive. For all the charms and joys of home, something isn't quite right. There's a flaw that none of us have been able to fix. No matter how beautiful it is to go home, it's never a place where we feel completely settled or at rest.

You know how it is when you go home after being away for a while. No sooner have you arrived than you get a desire to go somewhere else. Maybe you want to go shopping, or you have a sudden urge to see some of the old "haunts." Friends you haven't seen in a blue moon want to get together, so you ask if it's okay—not because you have to, but because you don't want to hurt anyone's feelings. Of course, they tell you it's fine, but deep down they're wondering why you don't stick around.

Then the time comes when you have to leave and get on with the business of your life, and you realize that as wonderful as home is, it isn't your final resting place. We don't mean to be morbid (especially at Christmastime), but there's something about the human heart that will never be at peace or at rest in any home on earth. C. S. Lewis said it best when he wrote:

> *If I find in myself a desire which no experience in this world can satisfy, the most probable explanation is that I was made for another world.*

This is not something to worry about. Just because you realize that "this world" will never be your true home doesn't mean you can't appreciate the blessings God has given you. A family that knows you and loves you, and a home—even though temporary— can fill you with joy. At the same time, be thankful that there is a final and truly ideal home in your future, where you'll be completely loved and perfectly known. That's when you will truly be able to say, "I'm finally home."

- "Home for the holidays" should be more than a slogan. It should be a goal.

- Whenever you are home, appreciate the blessings. When you are away, savor the memories.

- One of the best gifts you can give your family is to create a home they can enjoy.

- Because children are a gift from God, see them as guests rather than possessions.

- The way you treat your children when they are living with you will determine their desire to return when they are away.

The outdoor Christmas lights,
green and red and gold and blue and twinkling,
remind me that most people are
that way all year round—
kind, generous, friendly, and with
an occasional moment of ecstasy.
But Christmas is the only time
they dare reveal themselves.

HARLAN MILLER

THIRTY
LIGHTS

If you don't know your neighbors very well, you can at least get a glimpse into their personalities by the way they decorate the exteriors of their homes at Christmastime:

- How about that neighbor who never keeps up with her yard work? You've always thought that she was lazy and disrespectful of the neighborhood's pride of ownership. But at Christmastime, you notice that she's willing to endanger her life by standing precariously on the top rung of a ladder to string Christmas lights on the eaves of her house. If fact, she put her lights up right after Thanksgiving, while yours are still in the box in the attic. Maybe you've been too harsh in your assessment. Perhaps her yard is not unkempt after all; maybe it's just that she prefers natural overgrowth to manicured shrubbery.

- Then there's the guy who goes completely overboard with the lights. He has them strung over every angle of his roof, tacked to every window and doorframe, and wrapped around every pillar, tree, and plant. He must be intent on getting his house mentioned on the evening news—and he's contributing to the energy shortage in the process.

- And what about the neighbor—probably ex-military or an architectural engineer—who lives directly across the street from you, who arranges the light bulbs with exactitude? They are aligned perfectly and spaced evenly. It must have taken hours and involved the use of a protractor and a micrometer to achieve such precision. Your loopy strands of lights look pitiful by comparison.

Nobody knows how lights got to be such an integral part of the Christmas decorating tradition. Whatever the reason, secular or sacred, lights are engrained in the holiday's motif. While the derivation may be unknown, it isn't hard to find a logical connection to the story of Christ's birth: The star the wise men followed must have been a bright light, and the angels who surrounded the shepherds must have lit up the sky. But perhaps the best way to associate the tradition with the underlying story of Christmas is to consider what Christ said about Himself:

> *Jesus spoke to the people once more and said, "I am the light of the world. If you follow me, you won't have to walk in darkness, because you will have the light that leads to life."*

> JOHN 8:12

When Jesus said this, He was standing in the temple in Jerusalem where candles were burning. These candles represented the time in Jewish history when God took the form of a pillar of fire to lead the Israelites through their forty years in the wilderness. To the Jews, the pillar of fire symbolized God's presence, His direction, and His protection.

Notice that Jesus doesn't ask us to follow Him in darkness. He doesn't want us stumbling around in the mysterious shadows of life. He will be the light for us through our journey of life. He will provide the illumination that gives us a sense of safety. He will brighten our path so we can take the next step.

If you get depressed at Christmastime, or if you experience anxiety from all the holiday hubbub, try looking at decorative lights. They won't be hard to find. For you, those lights can symbolize God's guidance. He doesn't want you to feel alone in the darkness. He doesn't want you living in fear or uncertainty. He wants you to feel warmed and safe in His presence.

When you have a sense that God is the Light of Life, your entire outlook will change. Your life will be brighter. And, who knows? You just might become playful enough to tell your obsessive-compulsive across-the-street-neighbor that one of his bulbs is crooked. Just don't say which one.

. . .In the Small Stuff

- Don't worry if you can't see miles ahead on the path of your life. Just be assured that God will give you enough light for your next step.

- The One who came as the Light of the World is also the One who is the lamp for your path.

- It is permissible—even preferable—to leave the Light of Christmas shining all year long. (But the lights on the eaves of your house should be taken down by New Year's Day.)

- God's light can penetrate any darkness.

- Christ is the only Light that is its own renewable energy source.

- If you spread the Light of Christmas, you will contribute to global warming—and this will be a good thing.

Christmas is the gentlest, loveliest
festival of the revolving year—
and yet, for all that, when it speaks,
its voice has strong authority.

W. J. CAMERON

THIRTY-ONE

THE NATIVITY

The nativity is one of the best-known, most often told stories in history. Asked to describe the events surrounding Jesus' birth, most people could probably give the basic components of the story: An angel tells a young virgin she's going to give birth to the Savior of the world. . . . Mary and Joseph travel to Bethlehem, but there's no room in the inn. . . . They find shelter in a stable where Jesus is born. . . . Angels announce the good news to a bunch of shepherds, who run to see the baby Jesus. . . . Some wise men drop by to pay their respects and leave some gifts.

That's the nativity story in a nutshell—at least the one you'll see at your church's Christmas pageant, featuring children in bathrobes and fake beards.

As much we enjoy those charming pageants, we think those annual presentations sell the Christmas story short. Reducing God's great epic to a single stage with amateur actors and homemade props can't begin to capture its scope and grandeur. Truth is, the nativity is a massive and earth-shattering event that spans the unlimited time and space of eternity, featuring characters both visible and invisible. It's so grand and so powerful that any attempt—whether a church play or a Hollywood blockbuster—fails to express what it meant for God to relate to His human creation the way He did.

The plot itself is one for the ages, full of paradoxes and reversals. The tiny baby born on earth is actually a heavenly King. The birth is in the lowliest of places, and the human characters God recruits are humble people without status. Except for the wise men (who came two years after Christ's birth), those who take part in the story and then share it with others are from the bottom strata of society.

The greatest human writer could never invent such a wondrous story. It came to us directly from the mind of God, who through the nativity announced several truths to the world:

- The weak will be made strong;
- The lowly will be exalted;
- The poor in spirit will become spiritually rich;
- Those who mourn will be comforted;
- Those who are meek will inherit the earth; and
- Those who desire a truly good life will find it.

And it's all because Jesus came to the world on that first Christmas.

This is the heart of the nativity. It's a mystery revealed by God, centered in Christ, put into effect when the time was right. It's a story for the ages. It's not a story to watch like an audience watches a play—we can actually jump in ourselves, as characters with the opportunity to participate in all that the story means.

So the next time you see a nativity pageant in church, view it with this fresh perspective. Put yourself in the tableau, because God didn't write the story for just anyone. When it's all said and done, He did it for *you*.

- Support your church's nativity pageant. Though it can't begin to capture the grandeur of the real event, it does tell the story—and that counts for a great deal.

- Support Hollywood's attempt to tell the nativity story, even if they don't always get it exactly right.

- When you tell the nativity story to your children, be dramatic. After all, it isn't a fairy tale—this is God's great story.

- Be thankful that God uses the lowly to accomplish His purposes, because in comparison to His greatness, we are *all* lowly.

- Make the reading of the nativity story (from Matthew 1:18–2:21 and Luke 2:1–20) part of your Christmas traditions.

Probably the reason we all
go so haywire at Christmastime
with the endless unrestrained and
often silly buying of gifts
is that we don't quite know how
to put our love into words.

HARLAN MILLER

THIRTY-TWO

GIFTS AND GIVING

The tradition of Christmastime gift giving didn't begin when Jesus was born. Mary and Joseph may have marked the occasion of Christ's first birthday, but it wasn't celebrated with a gift exchange among the relatives and neighbors. The entire Christmas gift thing came hundreds of years later—and it probably wasn't rooted in the Christian faith. But we can still attach a spiritual significance to our own customs of giving and receiving gifts at Christmastime.

God gave the gift of His Son to all humanity that first

Christmas evening. In doing so, He established some principles of gift giving that provide good guidelines for us to follow:

The gift was exactly what we needed. One technical term describes a Christmas gift that nobody wants: *fruitcake*. But the category also includes Aunt Kim's gift of souvenir ashtrays to her nonsmoking niece and nephew; a necktie for Grandpa who only wears polyester jogging suits; and the box of See's candy you gave your pastor's wife, not knowing she was diabetic. God's gift, though, was specifically and uniquely what the human race needed—it was a gift designed and intended to cure our sin virus. God could have given other nice gifts (like heat without humidity or broccoli that tastes like chocolate), but anything less than a sacrifice for our sins would have left us in desperate need.

The gift wasn't what we were expecting. Often, a gift may meet a need, though it isn't what the recipient was hoping for. Just ask any teenager who gets socks for Christmas. Sure, you need things like socks and toilet paper, but no one puts them on their Christmas list. The same is true of the Jews in the first century (and all of humanity since, for that matter). They wanted a Messiah who would free them from Roman oppression, leading them into autonomy and prosperity. They weren't expecting a Messiah who would speak about the *spiritual* freedom that comes from an intimate relationship with God. That's exactly what those first-century Jews needed, but they had other things higher on their list. Still, God gave them what He knew would be best for them.

A sacrifice was involved. There may be nothing more disappointing on Christmas morning than receiving a gift that reveals a lack of effort on the part of the giver. Just ask a wife whose husband presents a stapled-shut bag from the Gas-N-Go; inside she finds a tin of breath mints, an assortment of candy bars, windshield wiper replacement blades, and an incriminating receipt indicating the purchase was made twenty-seven minutes earlier. In contrast, the most meaningful gifts are those that involve an obvious sacrifice by the giver. Balmy weather and candy-flavored vegetables would have been easy for God to conjure up. Such gifts might have been enjoyed by humanity, but the gifts would not have involved even the slightest inconvenience on God's part. Instead, He chose to send His Son to earth, knowing that Christ would be tortured and put to a brutal death. As the Bible says, "There is no greater love than to lay down one's life for one's friends" (John 15:13).

As you make your Christmas-shopping decisions, keep these principles in mind. Let your love for the recipient be reflected by a gift that is uniquely appropriate for that person. Give a gift that shows you made a sacrifice, not necessarily in money but in effort and thoughtfulness. And, whatever you do, don't Christmas shop at the Gas-N-Go.

- The statement is true: *It is not the gift but the thought that counts.* But it's also true that the gift usually reflects the amount of thought that was involved.

- A gift of your time and attention is more valuable than anything that can be wrapped.

- An inexpensive gift is irrelevant if the gift was thoughtfully chosen. A high price is meaningless if there was little thought involved.

- You've given a good gift if it conveys how well you know the recipient.

- Your appreciation is the gift you give back in return for a gift you have received.

Yet to all who received him,
to those who believed in his name,
he gave the right to become children of God.

JOHN 1:12 NIV

THIRTY-THREE

RECEIVING

Christmas is the season of giving. No one needs to tell you that, because this time of year every store and nearly every broadcasting station reminds you constantly that it's time to shop for gifts. And if you happen to miss the commercial clues, some of your closest friends and family members are more than happy to provide you with a list of suggested items they would love to receive.

You probably don't mind those attempts to inspire your giving. The old saying, "It's better to give than to receive," really is true. Giving is fun. Giving is fulfilling. What isn't as fulfilling is *receiving* gifts. That's not to say it isn't enjoyable, because it is. Opening presents is a blast, but our enthusiasm for what lies beneath the wrapping paper can quickly die, usually for one of two reasons.

One, the gift can turn out to be much less than you thought it would be. If this happens, it's important to maintain your cheery mood, even though you've just received a pair of oven mitts from Aunt Rose. Enthusiasm can also wane when you get a gift that goes way beyond what you expected—especially if you were "exchanging" gifts with another person. Elation can quickly turn to embarrassment, even resentment, if the gift puts you in an awkward position, such as feeling like you don't deserve it.

The point is this: Not only is it better to give than to receive, it's also easier. Receiving something—especially something you don't think you deserve—can be tough.

Perhaps you already know where we're going with this. It's one thing to receive a valuable earthly gift for which you feel unworthy. Imagine what it's like to receive a gift from heaven—a good and perfect gift—whose value is beyond measure. That's exactly what God asks us to do at Christmas, when we are reminded that He has given us the greatest gift of all, the gift of His Son. And just as an earthly gift can't be earned (otherwise it would be more like a bonus than a gift), neither can God's heavenly gift. It must be received.

Makes sense, doesn't it? At Christmas, what good is a gift left under the tree, unopened? It's pretty to look at, but it doesn't do any good. Only when you open and receive the gift does it serve the purpose for which it was intended.

Think about God's gift of Jesus for a minute. Have you "unwrapped" and received the Gift? Or have you left Him wrapped and lying in the manger, waiting for Christmas to pass so you can put Him away for another year? The apostle John, reflecting on the fact that Jesus was born into a world that did not receive Him, made the observation that *anyone* who receives the gift of life through God's Son would gain the right to become God's children—in effect adopted into God's eternal family as co-heirs with Christ.

There's nothing we could possibly do to be worthy of receiving God's great gift—it's based completely on His grace. But receive it we must, and what better time than Christmas?

. . .In the Small Stuff

- Receiving a gift is essential to the giving.

- Giving a gift is an option; receiving a gift is not.

- There's nothing more disappointing to a gift-giver than to know the gift was never received or opened.

- Thank God that He has given the gift of Jesus to everyone.

- If you've never received God's great Gift, there's no better time to do that than now.

Then Herod called for a private meeting with the wise men, and he learned from them the time when the star first appeared. Then he told them, "Go to Bethlehem and search carefully for the child. And when you find him, come back and tell me so that I can go and worship him, too!"

After this interview the wise men went their way. They returned to their own country by another route, for God had warned them in a dream not to return to Herod. Herod was furious when he realized that the wise men had outwitted him. He sent soldiers to kill all the boys in and around Bethlehem who were two years old and under, based on the wise men's report of the star's first appearance.

MATTHEW 2:7–9, 12, 16

THIRTY-FOUR

KING HEROD

The Bible doesn't tell us much about King Herod. But other Jewish and Roman historical accounts do. And it is not a pretty picture: King Herod was one messed-up dude.

Herod was only half Jewish, but he was politically connected—so he finagled an appointment as procurator of Judea. The job had a lot of perks, but also challenges. The foremost responsibility was to keep peace in the Jewish territory so that the high muckety-mucks in Rome could send the military to other regions. This was no easy task, because the predominant sentiment among the Jews was hatred of the Roman control over them. And Herod didn't make things any better—like when he assumed a phony title, "King of the Jews," which offended his constituency instead of gaining their favor. His rebuilding of the Jewish temple also backfired, when the insulted Jews saw him construct temples to pagan gods, too.

Political blunders weren't the least of his problems. King Herod was a madman—literally. His paranoia and fear of losing his position prompted him to assassinate anyone he perceived as a threat, including the high priest, many other priests, and various political opponents.

His psychological instability explains why King Herod reacted with such a heinous plan when the wise men rode into Jerusalem inquiring about the Messiah—the authentic King of the Jews. Herod wanted to trick the wise men into disclosing the whereabouts of this recently born ruler—so he could then have the baby murdered. But his plan was foiled when the magi discerned his evil intentions and never reported back after visiting

Mary, Joseph, and Jesus. (And maybe that's why we refer to them as the "wise" men.)

Although Herod and baby Jesus were both kings and only a few miles apart, the contrast between them was striking. The impostor king lived in opulence—but also in crushing paranoia. Meanwhile, Jesus—the real King—was born into humble and commonplace circumstances. There were no trappings of royalty around Him. He came to earth in the most vulnerable and dependent way. . .you can't get more helpless than being a baby. Even as an adult, Jesus never asserted His supernatural and divine power to advance His own cause or secure His entitlement to authority. Instead of demanding loyalty and allegiance by threat of force, He simply drew people to Himself by His kindness and wisdom.

Herod didn't realize that any attempt to interfere with God's plan will be futile. This puny pretender couldn't thwart God's will to install the genuine King of the Jews. Herod's most dastardly schemes and most devious plots could not prevail against God's divine eternal plan.

This provides solace when we're overwhelmed by events that seem out of control. In such times, we need to be reminded of God's sovereign power over the circumstances that swirl around us. God doesn't want us scheming and fretting. He doesn't want us asserting our independence and fighting the forces against us. Rather, He wants us to depend on Him. If He can protect a baby from the evil intentions of a king, don't you think He can protect you from the circumstances of your life?

- Replace the worry in your life with worship.

- Coming to your rescue is what God is good at.

- God wants to give you a gift of peace, but unwrapping the gift means letting Him take control.

- God is the perfect gentleman. He won't intervene in your life unless He's invited.

- God's power is a renewable energy source.

Crib and cross are both of the same wood.

HELMUT THIELICKE

THIRTY-FIVE

FORGIVENESS

In an earlier chapter we made the point that love is the *reason* we have Christmas. Now let's consider the *result* of Christmas. Love motivated God to send Jesus that first Christmas night. But as important as love is, it doesn't tell us everything about Jesus and why He came to earth in the first place.

"God loved the world so much that he gave his one and only Son" (John 3:16). That's the *reason* Jesus came to earth. But it's only one part of the story. The other part is the *result* of that love: "so that everyone who believes in him will not perish but have eternal life." In a word, the result of the love and the result of the story of Jesus is *forgiveness*—because that's what happens when we believe in God's Son. We are forgiven.

Early in the ministry of Jesus a paralyzed man was brought to Him for healing. The people who brought the man believed Jesus could heal their friend, and, because of their faith, Jesus did heal him—but not before He forgave the man of his sins. You see, the man's body wasn't the only thing that was paralyzed. His spirit was, too. That was the issue that concerned Jesus the most. Physical healing is for this life only, but spiritual healing is for eternity.

In more ways than one, we are like that paralyzed man. We come to Jesus thinking that our physical (or emotional) hurts are the big issue, but Jesus has something more to offer. He offers forgiveness. He *promises* forgiveness. Yes, Jesus wants to heal our hurts, but first He wants to forgive us. Without forgiveness (the *result* of Christmas) we cannot fully experience the love of God (the *reason* for Christmas).

Someone has said that the life of Jesus began in a stable

and ended on a cross. During this season of joy and love and peace and goodwill, it isn't exactly pleasant to think that the baby in the manger will grow up to suffer and die. Why does the Christmas story have to end that way? Because the cross is what makes Jesus' promise to forgive a reality. The truth is that the crib and the cross are both of the same wood. Without the birth of Jesus, there is no love. But without the cross, there is no forgiveness.

There's another dimension to forgiveness that will help you experience Christmas more fully. Just as God has forgiven you because of Jesus, you need to forgive others. There's no better time than now to think about those people who have offended you or harmed you in some way. Are you holding a grudge or cherishing bitterness toward anyone else? In the spirit of Christmas, where love and forgiveness stand like bookends on either end of the remarkable life of Jesus, you need to forgive.

Whenever we're tempted to be stingy with our forgiveness, we need to remember that in our relationship with God, we are the offenders and God is the offended. We have hurt God and don't deserve His forgiveness—but He made the first move toward us. Out of His deep love for us, through the death of Jesus, He forgives us—and He expects us to forgive others.

. . .In the Small Stuff

- Without forgiveness, there can be no healing.

- Without forgiveness, there can be no love.

- Without forgiveness, there is only the crib.

- The journey from the stable to the cross isn't an easy one, but it's a journey we must take.

- We should always value eternal benefits more than temporal ones.

After the wise men were gone, an angel
of the Lord appeared to Joseph in a dream.
"Get up! Flee to Egypt with the child
and his mother," the angel said.
"Stay there until I tell you to return, because Herod is
going to search for the child to kill him."
That night Joseph left for Egypt with
the child and Mary, his mother,
and they stayed there until Herod's death.

MATTHEW 2:13–15

THIRTY-SIX

EGYPT

Christmas occasions don't always turn out the way we would like. As we plan and anticipate, we envision everything going perfectly. *In our minds*, we see the immediate and extended family gathering in a festively decorated house on Christmas Eve—everyone is joyous and loving, and we all enjoy a sumptuous dinner, lingering for hours around the table to regale each other with stories from the past and updates of our current circumstances. *In our minds*, we experience the perfect Christmas.

But *in reality*, things don't turn out like that. When

Christmas Eve arrives, we notice the Christmas tree is brown because the stand is dry, the cat shredded the decoration hanging on the front door, and for some reason the sewer line backed up and all the toilets in the house are out of commission. But we hardly notice these minor irritations, because we're preoccupied with keeping our relatives from strangling each other. We're busy acting as referee, as old grudges return like mummies from the grave. Luckily, a few people aren't yelling—but they're sharing a long list of complaints about the dry turkey, the soggy vegetables, the sour eggnog, and the shredded front-door decoration. We're tempted to retreat to a safe place, but then we remember that the doors to the bathrooms have been nailed shut.

Let's face it. As much as we all love the Christmas season, the days often disappoint us—because reality turns out far differently than our expectations. But this disparity between expectation and reality is in keeping with the first Christmas. Imagine the range of emotions Mary and Joseph experienced. Despite the difficulties of travel on a very pregnant Mary, despite the lack of a suitable birthing place, despite all the fear and frustration caused by events and circumstances, worry turned to joy when a healthy baby boy—with all his fingers and toes and a good set of lungs—was born in that stable. Then, Mary and Joseph's joy turned to amazement as shepherds arrived in the nighttime hours to tell of an army of angels that confirmed that this newborn was God's long-promised Messiah. And, sometime after they were settled in Bethlehem, Mary and Joseph were awestruck at the arrival of wise men who presented gifts and worshiped the baby Jesus as a King. With these events as background, you can imagine that Mary and Joseph had certain expectations of their future—perhaps envisioning a life replete with God's blessing, honor, and privilege for their son.

But, just as with our lives, Mary and Joseph's reality turned out differently. As the story of the first Christmas comes to a close, the little family has to sneak out of town and cross the national border into Egypt. With Herod's decree to kill all the young boys, they have no choice but to leave their homeland.

This is no mere disappointment; this is true tragedy. Mary and Joseph make their escape as refugees to Egypt, not knowing if they will ever return to the land of Israel. Will they ever see their loved ones again? Will they ever again be able to worship in the temple in Jerusalem—or even practice their faith in Egypt? Will Joseph be able to find work? Is there a bounty on the head of their son? Will they be forced to live incognito, forever worried that Herod's henchmen are lurking behind every corner? The laughter and worship that filled their home in Bethlehem at the visit of the wise men quickly turned into worry, despair, uncertainty, and fear.

Suddenly, the problems with your relatives and plumbing don't seem so bad, do they? Here's the lesson for us, no matter how trivial or severe our unexpected Christmas complications: God didn't abandon Mary, Joseph, and Jesus in Egypt. In fact, He sent them there for their protection. God provided for them in Egypt, perhaps having them "cash in" the gifts from the wise men to subsidize their living expenses. And God later returned them to their hometown of Nazareth after Herod died. They were faithful in following God's direction, and God was faithful in directing their lives according to His will.

And so it will be with you. When God directs you to be the spirit of Christmas in your family, do it wholeheartedly—even though you know the reality may not match the expectations.

- The spirit of Christmas is best celebrated in your heart. It is safe there from the humbug attitude of others.

- The only place you'll have a perfect Christmas in is your mind. Anticipate that a few things will go wrong, and don't fret about them when they do.

- Don't let the details and logistics of your Christmas celebration distract you from the *reason* for the celebration.

- Expect the generosity of your Christmas spirit to be tested by those who don't have any.

- Don't let the disparity between expectation and reality ruin your Christmas. Enjoy the reality and try to see God in it.

Language has created the word *loneliness*
to express the pain of being alone,
and the word *solitude* to express
the glory of being alone.

PAUL TILLICH

THIRTY-SEVEN

LONELINESS

Have you ever noticed that Christmas and crowds seem to go together? When you go out to buy Christmas gifts, there's no escaping the hordes of shoppers. When you attend a special Christmas pageant or program, you're likely to encounter a "full house." When you imagine going home for Christmas, you can't help but think about all the friends and family members you are going to see—not to mention the busy highways you'll travel to get there.

It's not that you mind all the people. Crowds help to give

Christmas its unique character. Activity is part of the joy. Yet, for many people, the hustle and bustle of Christmas are anything but joyful. Far from being a time of celebration with others, Christmas can be a time of loneliness.

Being alone at Christmas can be painful, especially if you've recently experienced the loss of a loved one. Or you may find the presence and the pressure of crowds to be oppressing, causing you to withdraw to a solitary place. If you can identify with either of these reasons for loneliness, we've got some news for you: Jesus knows exactly what you're going through. Though He was God, Jesus became a human being so He could fully identify with you—and that includes identifying with your loneliness.

The Gospels tell the story of John the Baptist, a relative and close friend of Jesus. John was executed by King Herod, and when Jesus heard the news, the Bible says that "he left in a boat to a remote area to be alone" (Matthew 14:13). Jesus felt the pain of losing someone close to Him, and His natural reaction was to be alone. On several other occasions, the crowds of people who wanted to hear Jesus teach or feel His healing touch became so oppressive that He had to withdraw to a place of solitude. Jesus knew what it was like to feel the pressure of people, and His natural reaction was to be alone.

In fact, Jesus encouraged His followers to "get away," alone, from time to time. Once, Jesus' disciples came to report on their activities. No doubt they were eager to tell their leader how busy they were. As they were giving their reports, the crowds started pressing in, so much so that they didn't even have a chance to eat. With great wisdom, Jesus said to them, "Let's go off by ourselves to a quiet place and rest awhile" (Mark 6:31).

It's very possible that you are like those followers of Jesus the Bible talks about. Your life is full of activity. You love the crowds. You look forward to full houses, whether in a public place or your own home. That's great—but don't let your enjoyment of people be the only thing that characterizes your Christmas experience. In order to bring balance to your life, we would like to suggest that you do what Jesus did from time to time: withdraw from the celebration of crowds to embrace the contemplation of solitude.

As much as loneliness can be painful, solitude can be glorious—especially at Christmastime. If Jesus withdrew in order to rest, recharge, and pray, how can we do any less?

. . .In the Small Stuff

- Never underestimate the power of solitude.

- Far from being a curse, solitude can be a gift.

- You don't have to be a loner to feel alone at Christmas.

- Loneliness is a reminder that we need others; solitude is a reminder that we need God.

- Don't get alone with God just so you can get away from others; get away from others so you can get alone with God.

The best of all gifts around any Christmas tree:
the presence of a happy family all
wrapped up in each other.

BURTON HILLIS

THIRTY-EIGHT

FAMILY

There seems to be an inextricable connection between Christmas and "family." You can't think of one without bringing up memories of the other. Whatever the reason, we feel closest to our family at Christmastime. Each year, we're intent on making Christmas a family time to enjoy.

The concept works well when the household has a young child (or children) who awaken early on Christmas Day and dance excitedly in their pajamas around a pile of gifts. But as children grow older, the logistics for celebrating as a family unit become more difficult. As years go by, life circumstances make getting the entire family together at Christmas more challenging:

- The parents' divorce means that a child's Christmas may be spent with the noncustodial parent while the custodial parent is left alone.

- A child's enrollment at a faraway college creates a financial hardship that precludes returning home for the Christmas break.

- The marriage of a child raises the possibility that he or she will miss Christmas with parents because the holiday will be celebrated with in-laws. Maybe the best you can hope for is alternating years or trading Thanksgiving and two other holidays for Christmas.

- Jobs and careers may disburse families to distant locations, making a Christmas commute "back home" impractical.

- The death of a child may leave an empty place in the parents' home, a tragedy that's always more obvious and painful at Christmas.

- An elderly parent may live in a care facility, so joining the family celebration becomes an impossibility. The eventuality of death means a time will come when Christmas celebrations with parents are over forever.

None of these circumstances is pleasant to think about, but the likelihood of them (even the inevitability of some) is very real. Perhaps you're already experiencing one or more of these transitions. If so, you know the sense of loss that may be more prevalent on Christmas Day than any other time of the year.

Because of these ever-present possibilities threatening our family unity at holiday time, we should take every opportunity and make every effort to celebrate and appreciate each family Christmas gathering to the fullest. Petty differences need to be set aside; that hurtful, flippant remark made at the last Thanksgiving dinner should be forgotten; those guilty of offenses should be forgiven. Christmas is the time to celebrate the *best* of our family relationships, not dwell on the worst of them.

And because these same circumstances have already perpetrated loss in some family circles, we should expand our view of "family." The spirit of charity that pervades the season should encourage us to watch for people who have no family (or limited family) connections to draw upon at Christmastime. The "adoption" of one or two people—from your neighborhood or church—into your family for Christmas dinner may be the most tangible expression of God's love that you and they will experience. And if you're the lone soul without family this Christmas, God may give you special sensitivity toward those who are similarly situated, who would appreciate being invited to a group celebration you initiate.

Expanding your definition of *family* fits the Christmas model. God sent His Son to earth as Savior for the entire human race. That was an objectionable concept for first-century Jews who wanted to make an exclusive claim to the Messiah. They wanted Him for their Jewish family alone. But God's definition of *family* extended to Jews and non-Jews alike. He wasn't restrictive—the invitation to join His family extends to all, regardless of racial, economic, political, or social profiles. God opened His definition of *family* to include all of us—so it seems appropriate that we could take a similarly inclusive approach at Christmastime.

And, as Dickens' Tiny Tim said so memorably, "God bless us, every one!"

- The first Christmas was a family celebration. Keep that tradition.

- God was willing to include you in His family. Follow His example by inviting others to join yours.

- The joy you experience at Christmas can grow in direct proportion to the number of people who celebrate with you.

- Do you want to teach your children the real meaning of Christmas? Set a few extra places at the Christmas dinner table, and fill them with people who would otherwise be alone for the holiday.

- You'll never be without "family" at Christmas if you're willing to expand your definition of the term.

"Glory to God in highest heaven,
and peace on earth to those with
whom God is pleased."

LUKE 2:14

THIRTY-NINE

PEACE

There's a lot of talk about peace at Christmas. Even those who don't care much about Christmas as a celebration of Jesus' birth like to promote peace at this time of year. You could say that Christmas is the season of peace for the whole world.

Of course, if the newspaper headlines are any indication, there's not much peace going on in the world, whether it's across the seas or in your own town. It may be Christmas on the calendar, but bombings, murders, kidnappings, and all sorts of bad stuff are still happening everywhere you look. Even if you don't focus on the violence, you find arguments, strife, and disharmony in your workplace, your neighborhood, maybe even your home.

So what's all this "peace on earth" business the angels announced that first Christmas? Was it all hype? If there would never be peace in the world, why did the prophet Isaiah give God's Son the title "Prince of Peace" and predict that "His government and its peace will never end" (Isaiah 9:6–7)?

For the answer, take a look at the *entire* announcement the angels gave that holy night:

> *"Glory to God in highest heaven, and peace on earth*
> *to those with whom God is pleased."*
>
> LUKE 2:14

It isn't peace for the whole world, but only for those God favors—in other words, those who have put their trust in Jesus and committed themselves to Him. Jesus explained the nature of this peace when He told His followers, "I am leaving you with a gift—peace of mind and heart. And the peace I give is a gift the world cannot give. So don't be troubled or afraid" (John 14:27).

This kind of internal serenity transcends the external peace everyone hopes for at Christmas. Though the storms of life rage around us, we can have calm assurance that our mighty and loving God has us firmly in His hand—*if* we have a personal relationship with the One who came to bring peace to the world.

This also explains Isaiah's prophecy about a "government and its peace" that will never end. All those who put their trust in Jesus become part of His spiritual Kingdom—His government—where Jesus is not only Savior, but also Lord. This peaceable Kingdom ever expands as more and more people discover God's good news for themselves.

Meanwhile, as Christ's followers, we are to do all we can to bring peace—both spiritual and physical—to the world. The Bible tells us, "Do all that you can to live in peace with everyone" (Romans 12:18). Of all people in the world, those with God's peace in their hearts should be the most intentional about promoting peace. Just like the angels, we should proclaim and embody peace on earth, because we are the ones upon whom God's favor rests. It's both our privilege and our responsibility.

. . .In the Small Stuff

- God blesses those who work for peace.

- Jesus is the "Prince of Peace" in every way: He brings peace to all who follow Him, and someday He will bring peace to the world.

- There is no such thing as true peace apart from God.

- When you have the peace of God, you won't necessarily be comfortable—but you will be content.

- Christmas is a time of peace because it is a time for Christ.

There has been only one Christmas—
the rest are anniversaries.

W. J. CAMERON

FORTY

CELEBRATION

In one sense, Christmas Day never catches anyone by surprise. We don't need a desk calendar to know when it will occur. We may be unsure about the day of the week on which it will fall, but there is a 100 percent certainty that it will land on December 25. That single date becomes the target of our best and most intense feelings of generosity. Thoughts of "peace on earth" and our spirit of joy and goodwill toward others are released almost simultaneously with the celebration of Christmas.

But what about the rest of the year?

Why do we seem to hold the spirit of Christmas in reserve from January through November, only to be released when the calendar page flips to December? Why are we likely to be generous and charitable around Christmastime, but more tightfisted the rest of the year? (There must be more to it than the year-end deduction deadline for charitable contributions.) Why do we emphasize family togetherness on Christmas Day but try to avoid our relatives the remaining 364 days each year? Why do we give God a prominent role at Christmastime but hardly notice Him the rest of year?

Doesn't it seem that the best of humanity comes out in December, while the worst of what we are is suppressed during the Christmas season? On the other hand, during the eleven remaining months of the year, we expose our worst qualities while our best ones are conspicuously absent. It's as if we hold our good nature in reserve—like we only have a limited amount of it— saving it up to let it out at Christmastime.

Imagine how your life—and the lives of people you impact—would be different if you celebrated the Christmas spirit all year long:

- Every day, the atmosphere in your home would be more positive.

- You'd give gifts to your friends and family for no other reason than your affection for them. (Caution: This may make certain people nervous or suspicious.)

- You might serve meals at the soup kitchen each month, when your help was really needed, instead of on Christmas Day when the volunteers outnumber the homeless.

- You would attend church more than just once a year. (Think of the benefits: The parking lot won't be so crowded. . .there will be plenty of empty seats to chose from. . .and, for a change of pace, you'll get to hear a Bible passage that isn't the Christmas story.)

- You'd make contributions to charitable organizations in months when their cash flow is tight, rather than adding to the surplus that arrives in December.

- You could be especially courteous to store clerks during the Memorial Day sales when the rest of the customers are rude and cranky.

- You'd catch yourself humming Christmas carols in July (and that's not a bad thing).

Because the spirit of Christmas seems to bring out the best in us, shouldn't we celebrate beyond the parameters of December? If Christmas makes us feel better about ourselves and care more about others, why should we repress that spirit from January through November?

If you need an example of the transformation that Christmas can make, think of the classic literary character Ebenezer Scrooge. He had the humbug scared out of him and the spirit of Christmas scared into him. After his transformational dream, he said, "I will honor Christmas in my heart, and try to keep it all the year."

Once you try it, you'll probably decide that living Christmas all year long is a great idea. But don't get so wrapped up in the concept that you forget to take down your outdoor Christmas decorations. If you hum carols throughout the year, you might be considered eccentric—but if you keep your lights up past the holiday season, you could very well incur the wrath of your neighbors. They aren't as likely to have the Christmas spirit in July.

- Considering the underlying meaning of Christmas, it's an occasion that deserves a year-long celebration.

- Beat the Christmas rush. Send out your cards in September.

- Don't cram your Christmas shopping into the month of December. As you do your regular shopping throughout the year, look for gifts for the people on your Christmas list.

- If you buy Christmas gifts months in advance, you better remember where you hid them.

- Christmas should be put in your heart, not merely on the calendar.

"Go into the world.
Go everywhere and announce
the Message of God's good news to one and all."

MARK 16:15 THE MESSAGE

FORTY-ONE

GO TELL IT

From the moment Jesus was born, a whole bunch of people (and more than a few angels) were singing His praises—and they haven't stopped since. As you've read through this book, we hope you've learned why that's the case.

The birth of Jesus that first Christmas wasn't just any birth, because Jesus wasn't just any person. He was God in human form, sent to earth by His heavenly Father so that God could establish a personal and eternal relationship with anyone who would receive the gift of His Son. That's the good news of Christmas. Indeed, it's the good news of the Bible.

Something about good news makes it impossible to keep it to yourself. When you discover something that changes your life, you are compelled to share it with others.

- That's what happened that first Christmas night. The first to tell others about Jesus were the angels. The angelic beings are called "God's messengers" for a reason: They are the ones God uses to make big announcements.

- The angels made their big announcement about the birth of Jesus to the shepherds, who in turn ran all around Bethlehem telling people what they had seen and heard. (We suspect they caused quite a ruckus, being shepherds and all.)

- The last official Christmas messengers were the wise men. Even though they didn't see Jesus until two years later, their enthusiasm was just as contagious. After they returned to their homeland, they undoubtedly told everyone what they had seen.

All kinds of people—from common laborers to people of high standing—were engaged in telling others that Jesus Christ was born. How appropriate! You see, Jesus didn't come for certain kinds of people—He came for everyone. Throughout His life on earth, Jesus touched every kind of person: poor and rich, young and old, Jew and Gentile, woman and man, ruler and oppressed. And when He left earth to return to His heavenly home, He told His followers to continue His work—by going everywhere to tell everyone the message of God's good news.

Jesus may have been born two thousand years ago, but His presence is just as real today as it was when He physically walked the earth. He is still touching lives, still changing hearts.

Go, tell it on the mountain,
Over the hills and everywhere
Go, tell it on the mountain,
That Jesus Christ is born.

Just like the angels, the shepherds, and the wise men, that is our mandate. And it shouldn't be one that we fulfill just because we have to. When we think about all that Jesus did for us on that first Christmas night, we should be motivated to tell everyone we know that Jesus was born two thousand years ago, and He continues to be born again today in the hearts of people everywhere.

- The best way to show Christ to the world is to love others as He did.

- It's one thing to tell about Jesus with your words—it's much better to tell about Him with your life.

- Here are the last instructions Jesus gave before returning to heaven: "Go into all the world and preach the Good News to everyone, [everywhere]" (Mark 16:15).

- If you're nervous to tell someone about Jesus, remember that He promises to be with you.

- Let the shepherds be your example. They didn't have any theological credentials. They just told people about their personal encounter with Christ.

About the Authors

Bruce Bickel lives in the Pacific Northwest and Stan Jantz lives in Southern California. Despite the geographic distance between them, they have written more than sixty books together. They are the authors of the *Christianity 101®* series and the bestselling and award-winning *God Is in the Small Stuff. . .and it all matters.*

You can find out more than you want to know about Bruce and Stan and their other books at www.Christianity101Online.com

If the information on the Web site doesn't dissuade you from contacting them, you can e-mail the guys directly at Info@Christianity101Online.com.